I0133585

The Einstein Principle

The Einstein Principle

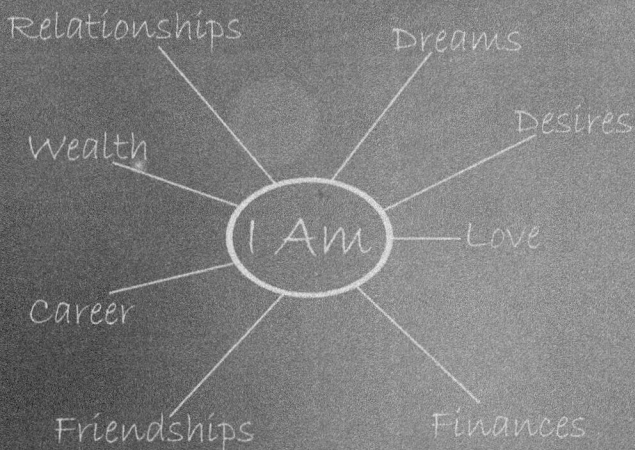

Relationships

Dreams

Desires

Wealth

I Am —— Love

Career

Friendships

Finances

How the Smartest Man in the World +
20,000 Psychic Readings Taught Me the
Secret to True Wealth & Happiness.

Michael E. Peterson

The Einstein Principle: How the Smartest Man in the World + 20,000 Psychic Readings Taught Me the Secret to Wealth & Happiness © 2015 by Michael E. Peterson. All rights reserved. No part of this book may be used or reproduced in any manner whatsoever, including Internet usage, without written permission from the author.

FIRST EDITION
First Printing, 2015

Book design: D. B. Brown
Developmental editor: Annie Wilder
Copyeditor: Sally Heuer
Cover art: Michael E. Peterson
Cover design: Michael E. Peterson
Interior illustrations: Michael E. Peterson

Library of Congress Cataloging-in-Publication Data
ISBN: 978-0-9965705-0-3

Printed in the United States of America

Contents

Thank you to my editor Annie Wilder at Annie Wilder's Inkswiggler Editing & Publishing Consults, and her fantastic team, Donna (graphic design) and Sally (copyeditor)—outstanding professional people that made the entire process seem so easy!

To my wife, Shelly, because without her love and support this would never have seen the light of day.

To Dave Grohl for being such an outstanding role model with an unstoppable work ethic.

To the Foo Fighters whose music always encouraged me to keep plugging away even when I wanted to stop.

To my family and friends who stood with me all these years; your support is forever in my heart.

Introduction

- Do you want to find the love of your life? Or rekindle passion and romance if you're already in a committed relationship?
- Do you want to create more harmonious relationships in your life?
- Do you want to increase your financial well-being?
- Do you want to change or further your career?
- Do you want to have control of your life instead of the other way around?

You CAN create the life you desire. I'm going to show you how. I have helped thousands of people transform their lives and make their innermost dreams come true.

My name is Michael. I want to share my life story with you and describe some of the pivotal experiences on my journey from childhood to this moment, leading to the creation of this book.

Don't be alarmed or discouraged if you answered yes to the questions at the beginning of this introduction. That only shows that you are among the millions of people who are experiencing difficulties of one nature or another in life right now.

However, there is a huge difference between you and those other millions of people. Right now, you are making conscious choices and decisions to make your life better. The other millions—well, it is obvious they either do not want to change, do not know how to change, or enjoy life as it is.

It does not matter where you are in life right now. It does not matter what job you have. The only thing that matters is that you have an honest-to-God desire to make your life better. As long as you have that, you can create positive, dynamic change in your life.

I was born outside of Detroit, Michigan, in 1968. Much to my surprise, my psychic gifts and talents emerged in my life in 1973 when I turned five years old, as I became clairaudient, clairvoyant, and clairsentient. I began to see loved ones who had passed away. I listened to messages they asked me to relay to other family members, which I did. That seldom went over well, mostly resulting in my family thinking I was strange, making things up, or both. I would talk with these spirits for hours at times, with my older brother thinking I had great imaginary play friends. However, it took the better part of the next decade for me to realize that very few people experienced the same things I saw, heard, and felt. Those ten years were confusing, scary, and chock-full of trying to find my place in the world.

There was no one to help me find my way or explain what was happening. The subject of ghosts, visions, premonitions, and anything of the spirit world was labeled taboo, or worse, occult. That last word was enough to scare any kid. The worldwide web had not been invented at that time, and the local library was a scattershot of information, more miss than hit.

During that ten-year stretch of what seemed like eternity, there were two very significant questions to which I strived to find answers. The first was, "Am I insane, or is what I am experiencing real?" The second question was, "If this is all real, does it fit with my religious beliefs, or is it coming from somewhere 'bad'?"

My first question was answered in 1984, when I was sixteen years old. I was in my mother's home talking with a very good friend of mine about everyday life. In the middle of our conversation, I began telling him what I had been shown, the mistreatment he received at the hands of his stepfather and things much more personal for him.

This went on for almost ten minutes, during which time I never looked up at him, I just continued speaking. When I finished relating what I had seen, I looked up. His face was deathly white, as if all the color had drained down into his toes. All he could say was, "I've never told you that. I've never told anyone that." He picked up his car keys and left. I didn't see him again for a long time. In that short time span, due to fear and misunderstanding, I had been alienated from a good friend.

For me, that cemented the fact that what I was seeing, hearing, and experiencing was very real and also very scary. It meant that all the fun and games were over, that I had to learn more about what I was doing. I never wanted to repeat what had happened, blurting out personal information that could create an adverse reaction such as pain, embarrassment, or fear.

I graduated from high school in the summer of 1986. I was married in the spring of 1989. Without doubt, my life had changed, but I continued to help people, answering their questions, passing along messages from deceased loved ones. All the while, I was trying to find more information about who I was becoming, and where this information—the visions, all of it—was coming from. The second question was still unresolved, and being married with a child, it became more pressing than ever to find an answer.

The fall of 1994 was when the next huge shift occurred in my life: I found my mentor. AOL Online was popular at the time, and I discovered Richard in an online chat room. I had entered a search for a metaphysical chat room and then left my PC to get something to drink. When I returned, I had been placed in a chatroom that had something like "Lighthouse" in the title. As I scrolled down the screen, just glancing at the conversation as it was happening, words began to jump out at me: *spirit, second sight, spiritual projection,* and more. At first I attributed my being directed to that particular chat room to coincidence, but I have since learned better. Over the course of the next month, I began to actively search for this man, Richard, in many online chat rooms. Often, when I found him online, I would just sit and read the conversations as they unfolded.

What Richard was speaking about to other people was exactly what I needed to learn. I must have been in many chat rooms with him every night for eight or nine weeks before we had properly introduced ourselves and exchanged phone numbers. Over the course of the next four years, my long-distance phone bill was astronomically high. There were many hours of late-night conversations and lively debates. I learned about the power of spoken word, the importance of intent and desire, and the reality of manifestation. Richard was able to help me understand the gravity of being a psychic, and the immense responsibility that went with it.

This man helped me refine my understanding of what was happening and taught me how to clear my mind and "listen" or "see" better. During those years, my psychic gifts and talents expanded, allowing me to read for people with a much more refined approach and to deliver clearer messages because I was picking up more detailed insights, deeper emotions, and more specific information that related just to them. Richard was the one who threw a wedge into the doorway that led to the psychic realm, a door that was barely open at that time. Over the coming years, I would be able to fling that door wide open.

I learned more than I can explain to people, and I had truly changed. I found I had changed beyond the comfort levels of my marriage, which led to my divorce in 1997.

Later that same year, I went to work for a company that required extensive travel. I began traveling to out-of-the-way places throughout the United States as well as most of Canada. In the spring of 1999 I married Shelly, a shift in my life for which I am more thankful than most people will ever know.

From 1997 to late in 2002, at every location I traveled to for work, I came across another person, or group of people, seeking guidance. I began reading for individuals with a wide variety of vocations, backgrounds, and social statuses. Complete strangers would often turn into friends, people I would continue to help for months afterward.

During this time, I began to take notes, keeping a journal of the readings as well as my thoughts and experiences. Some of the readings were humorous, due to the way the information came out or the way people reacted to the news. Others were inspiring and transformative, as I watched people absorb the information and then make instantaneous, life-altering changes. There were times when the readings were painful but also healing and comforting, relating very moving messages from the other side to loved ones in the here and now.

As I continued to do personal readings (what I began to call my real work) in those five years, I started to see some very important trends. It reminded me of looking at a jigsaw puzzle that someone dumped on the table. As I turned new pieces over, I separated them into categories, just like many people look for edge pieces to begin putting a puzzle together. The more I investigated things, conducted readings for people, and passed along spiritual messages, the more this giant puzzle began to take shape. At first I was skeptical of what I was seeing in my own writings, thinking my personal observations were coloring what I was putting in my notes. However, as time went on, I would learn that was not so.

In my journals, a stark fact was staring me in the face: people faced with similar challenges in life reacted in very similar ways. These responses, or patterns, were repeated consistently in matters of love, relationships, finances, and career issues. (These are the four main topics that many psychics deal with in the vast majority of their readings, and yes, they are listed in order of importance.) The rate at which I began finding these similarities when I reviewed my journals was shocking. The pattern was that, when faced with an issue or crisis in life, people reacted in very similar ways, meaning they were experiencing predictable outcomes. Unfortunately, very often they got results that they did not desire. Around this time, I stumbled across an observation made by one of the greatest minds of our time, the physicist Albert Einstein, which would impact my life like nothing I had read before. It was the quote that I came to think of as the Einstein Principle.

The quote attributed to Einstein is: "The world we have made as a result of the level of thinking we have done thus far creates problems that we cannot solve at the same level of thinking at which they were created." Searching for more information on this led me to a simplified version of the quote, which I use to this day: "Problems cannot be solved by the same level of thinking that created them." Only hours later, while I reviewed my journals again, I had an epiphany of how this principle beautifully illustrated the connection between nearly all of my readings. It was the catalyst for the book you now hold in your hands.

In the spring of 2000, my work travels brought me to the next major turning point in my life. The night before the national dedication of the Oklahoma City National Memorial, the city opened it to the local public, allowing them time to experience the memorial before the national media descended on it. I had the honor of being allowed to attend. As I spent time walking through the amazing memorial, all I could do was cry. It was emotionally overwhelming. I saw and heard so many things, both on a physical and spiritual level. It shook me to the core of who I am, leaving a profoundly deep impact.

Before the week was through, and after more than twenty years of searching, I was presented the answer to my second question about experiencing psychic abilities—"If this is all real, does it fit with my religious beliefs, or is it coming from somewhere 'bad'?" I was able to speak with a longtime friend and pastor, someone I trusted with my life, and I opened up about what was happening to me. Our conversation led to my asking, "Am I doing something that goes against my faith?"

The pastor's answer was short and to the point. "No. You've been given a gift and responsibility. I can't begin to try and understand it all, but as long as you walk in God's light, you remain a good man." As I left his office, I knew my life had changed again. At the age of thirty-two years old, for the first time ever, it was okay to be me.

In mid-2002, after being on the road during the tragedy and horror of September 11, I felt it was time to change jobs, and bring myself home to be closer to my wife and children. I had been away from home for far too long. I took a significant cut in pay and went to work for a company associated with large automakers, continuing my career in the information technology field.

For the next five years, as I continued doing my real work, I fleshed out my hypothesis of why people were caught in similar patterns and outcomes that often resulted in failure. The fuzzy picture I had been working on was becoming clearer, more defined, and much more real. It seemed that every reading I did added more clarity to the entire picture that was being shown to me.

The struggle of maintaining a career for someone else while trying to do more of my real work became seriously taxing. It felt like I was being ripped in two. I wanted to devote myself to my spiritual work all day every day, but I had bills to pay, and my day job was becoming more difficult. I was so focused on trying to maintain both my spiritual path and my regular job that it created issues in my marriage. My wife and family were feeling the pressure, which I had sworn would never happen again in my life.

In 2007, after talking with Shelly and giving things very serious consideration, it became painfully obvious that I needed to transition away from my "day job" and set my sights on following my true vocation. Accordingly, my day job came to an abrupt end. Within thirty days, I began working for an online company, where I was able to pursue my real vocation. I was reading for people on the phone for my new company, traveling to read for people at public events, and offering public speaking events, classes, and seminars.

This was a major shift in my life. I began to apply my years of experience to my own life, walking the talk. My life, my marriage, and my family were beginning to prosper and grow. In my work with the online company, I spoke with thousands of people from more than eighteen countries around the world. I once again experienced the true meaning of the word wealth, and trust me, it encompasses more than just money. Reading for so many people from all over the world, with so many types of backgrounds, jobs, and vocations, the picture I was shown of how to create the life of your dreams was validated time and again. It was one of the most exciting periods in my life.

I was able to take my writings from initial ideas and observations to practical, proven, and powerful advice for the real world. Along with the metaphysical aspect of reading for people, I began to employ my understanding of the Einstein Principle that I had been working on for the previous decade. This combination has since helped those thousands of people around the globe. What I learned can now be shared with many other people to help them change their life.

All of this personal history brings us to the present, right now.

From this point on, you and I are going have a rather long conversation.

You see, no matter how many books are published, no matter how many people might be reading this, right now (and for the remainder of this book), I will be speaking directly (as well as indirectly) with you. Without you, this is nothing more than a collection of paper and ink.

The whole reason I am writing this is to help bring very real changes into your life. I want to provide you those key insights I have found, the ones I have used to help other people around the globe. I want to help you to not only get to the next level in your life, but surpass it. I can give you the tools, insights, and understanding to help you change your life, to experience the true wealth I spoke of earlier.

From this point on, chapter after chapter, you and I are going to begin a discussion that will, with a little effort, change your life. Through our time together, we will walk through what I have learned.

In Section One, Chapters 1 through 4, I will show you *how* to create the life you desire. In each chapter, I will present a proven principle, a true case file from my professional psychic readings that will help illustrate that principle, some simple yet powerful interactive homework assignments, and a summary of the principle and lesson in the chapter.

In Section Two, which includes chapters 5 through 8, will tell you *why* the Einstein Principle works, providing an in-depth look at the physics behind the plan. Case files from my journals will also be provided to help in the understanding of the eternal connection between the physical world and the spirit world.

An appendix provides additional helpful tips as you embark on your new path, and free downloadable PDFs of helpful charts and material from this guidebook can be found on my website: www.mepeterson.com.

Each chapter is a step up and forward to creating a life born of your desires, every one of them integral to creating true wealth and prosperity. Each area in life is balanced on another, and if they are not aligned, well, then life can (and will) fall apart.

We will start with your particular goal or dream, the one that created within you the true desire for change. It could be to have a better career, to become a more loving spouse, to create a bigger balance in your bank account. Our conversation will touch on all of these and other areas in life, giving us a better understanding of what *true wealth* actually is, and means, and how it will help turn your dreams into your reality.

As long as you remain true to your desire to create a better life, then there are no limits to what you will achieve.

With all of this said, let's start walking on the path called change.

Section One

ONE

Real Change, Real Meanings

People always ask me, "What is it like to be psychic?" I love that question because it allows me to respond with, "What is it like to be normal?"

You see, since I spent the last forty-one years being the way I am now, I honestly don't have a frame of reference to answer "What is it like to be psychic?" because I have no clue what it is like to be normal. All I know is this is the way I am, and to me, I am normal. This is how my life has always been. I am very sure that at some point in time there will be that one person who can explain, in great detail, what it is like to be normal. At that point, I am also sure I will be able to describe what it is like to be psychic.

In forty-one years, I have come to grips with the fact that many people can neither hear nor see the things I do. I've also learned it's not a handicap, just a simple matter of perception. I happen to perceive things differently. It does not make me any better, or worse, than any other human on the planet. Just different.

However, now that you and I are going to begin our conversation, we need to develop a helpful framework for understanding, a way to bridge the gap between my perceptions of the metaphysical and the everyday perceptions of the physical world.

You and I will create an area in your perception within which you can begin to see things the way I do. No, this is not a course designed to turn you into a psychic. This is a subtle shift in your perceptions, one that allows you to think outside the box. For me, The Einstein Principle means that *problems cannot be solved by the same level of thinking that created them.* Thus, to begin to change your life, we have to begin to open your mind to a different perception, one of the metaphysical universe.

First, metaphysics is actually a division of philosophy, one that explores the fundamental nature of reality and perception while at the same time being an abstract philosophical study of phenomena that is outside objective experience.

In short, metaphysics is a study in theoretical knowledge of reality that is unexplained by science. The term and the actual philosophy have been around for more than 2,300 years. Since the time of Aristotle in 384 B.C., philosophers have devoted their entire lives to trying to prove or disprove that there is something outside of the physical.

Thankfully for us, we are not going to devote that kind of time to the topic. Right now, let's continue to build our framework that will allow us to communicate effectively and bridge the esoteric with down-to-earth thinking. We're going to discuss ideas, concepts, and experiences beyond the physical world, outside of our conventional day-to-day reality.

Before you become uneasy, think about this. Take a single word, *love.* It is not something science can explain; it is an emotion. It has no physical form, there is no way to measure it, nor can it be seen. We often experience the effects of the emotion, or see the results of it in action, but it remains intangible. Thus, it is an item that belongs to metaphysics, something beyond the physical world. Yet, that single emotion can have great cause and effect, moving people to do heroic things and making us cry tears of joy.

Because we labeled it a metaphysical item, did we diminish (or cheapen) the emotion? No, we just changed our perception of what it is, how it fits into our *physical* world. Love remains the same as it was; we just see it slightly differently now.

The next portion of creating our framework is to begin to put distance between some groups of words. For instance, take the words *possible* and *impossible*. I have no desire to play word games; just think about these words. Let's place some distance between *impossible* (a very negative word) and *possible* (a very positive word).

By placing enough distance between them in our thinking, this will allow us room to become hypothetical—enough room so that we do not jump from one word to the other while we talk with each other. We need that working space to begin to expand our vocabulary and allow room for *what if* and *maybe* types of thoughts. Without that space, there is no reason to continue reading; you might as well put the book down and stop wasting our time.

Remember, Einstein said we couldn't find answers to our problems using the same thinking we did when we created them. It's time to find a new way of thinking, which is where our framework comes into being and takes shape in our lives.

Just like possible and impossible, try putting some distance in your thinking of *right* and *wrong*. These are labels that hold absolute power in them, having the ability to either allow thoughts to continue or to throw them into the trash bin. There might be many ways to do something *wrong* but only a few ways to do something *right*.

Since we are going to explore thoughts, ideas, and subjects that are outside the norm, let's make some room to talk about them before your mind jumps into "Well, that's just plain wrong." A label quickly added to something often finds trouble. So, for our conversation, let's give some latitude to what we will speak about before jumping into right and wrong.

The last pair of words, very much like *right and wrong,* might be the most difficult to separate in your mind. I know it was for me. I spent six months arguing with my mentor about the two words, and I spent six months looking for aspirin. The reason it seems to cause such a problem is due to our everyday use of them. What we need to do, right now, is to create some breathing room for the words *good* and *bad.* I know, it seems contrary to so many other thoughts in your mind, but this one is very integral to our framework. Let me help you out with this one.

Think of a typical stone, something you might pick up by the lakeshore. In itself, the stone is neither good nor bad. If it has a beneficial property to it, we tend to label it *good,* and if it were thrown and hit someone, we might label it *bad.* However, the stone has no intrinsic value, positive or negative. It simply is. Nothing more, nothing less. The same thing needs to happen with parts of our conversation. We need space to think about things before we apply a powerful label of *good* or *bad.*

Once a connotation is given, our mind is going to stick with that until proven otherwise. Because we are dealing with things outside the physical world, it might become difficult to remove that label once attached. So please, for right now, let's use those words sparingly, and only when we know something concrete. Allow yourself to work within some gray areas for a short time, while we create some different ways of thinking.

With those simple things in place, our framework for conversations is complete. We now have a space to talk about many subjects, discuss many things, without the automatic instinct to say, "That's impossible" or "Oh, that is just wrong" or "That's bad." I'm not asking you to suspend your personal belief system—far, far from it. I am only asking that while you and I are talking, you give our conversation the space to be in our reality for a little while before you cast judgments or preconceptions on it.

It's all right to think of things as *hypothetical* for a little while; that works just as well. A *hypothesis* is a proposed explanation that we make knowing we have limited evidence to support our claim, yet we use it as a starting point for further investigation and conversation. Again, let's change our way of thinking in order to think of new answers to our old problems. That is exactly what we are doing right now.

Professional Case File

* All names have been changed to protect the privacy of the client
Date: 1998
Client: Shannon
Location: Pennsylvania

Our appointment began with Shannon lightly explaining her reasons for contacting me, which included a need to understand her fiancé Gerald's sudden postponement of their upcoming wedding (with no future date given) as well as to try to determine the next step in her career.

After mere minutes of speaking about Gerald, I was overcome with an emotional tidal wave of insecurity, self-doubt, and the compulsion to "go hide." I knew these were the emotions being felt by Gerald, as they left me almost as suddenly as they were presented to me.

In speaking with Shannon, we discussed Gerald's emotions as well as his tendency to seemingly back away and become a hermit at times. She admitted they had spoken of his fear that he might let her down financially, that he was afraid he might not be "the man's man" he so desperately wanted to be for her. She had assumed that the matter was settled, since they had spoken of it, and did not know why it had cropped up again. The insight I was given was to relay this: "Gerald has never known a love like yours in his entire life. He is very afraid of hurting you if he were to try something new and fail. His thought is that you would be better off with another man than risk taking this step with him." Shannon agreed to speak with Gerald on a much more intimate level, building new layers of trust.

As for her career, she explained she was in the middle of looking at three options for advancement, two of which were outside the company in new positions with competitors. She was unsure which might result in the best outcome for her, stating she had difficulty making choices with the wedding postponed.

The small movie clip that began playing in my mind's eye showed her in a work environment in which all the sights, sounds and environment were familiar to her, speaking with people as normal co-workers would and not in the careful way of someone with a new job and new colleagues. I conveyed this information to Shannon, stating that it appeared she would remain with her current employer. I remember the frustration in her voice as she outlined the three options.

Taking a few minutes to work with her to determine the real reasons why she desired the change in her life brought about a new clarity for her. Shannon was not so much worried about the raise she might get (a response which conflicted with her logical thinking), but she was only trying to determine which position would represent the most job security in the long run. Working together, we discovered this was the most important thing to her for one reason: to take care of Gerald in case something ever happened.

Personal notes included:

- Shannon was able to change her perception of why Gerald had seemingly run away from her and reaffirmed that she genuinely wanted them to renew their commitment to each other.
- She gained an understanding of the real reason why she desired change in her career. This was the key for her to take the confident next step in her career.
- Shannon and Gerald were married eight months later in a downsized wedding.

- A note from Shannon in 2009 reported that she and Gerald were happily married and had more financial success than either could explain.

This case file represents the importance of one's need to know the reasons for change. Knowing the why allowed Shannon to overcome her doubts about her relationship and discover the underlying reasons for deciding which job would be the best fit in her life.

Our Lesson—Part One

Shannon found that the famous line from Shakespeare's *Hamlet*, "To thy own self, be true," was vastly important to her life also. This is the one thing, above any other item in this entire work, that I will ask you to adhere to. Truth is a massive powerhouse, one that makes or breaks people. For you and me, being true to your self is *the* essential ingredient to your success. To help put our conversation into gear, let's test-drive this sentence: the wrecking ball has already been through your life and done some heavy-duty damage. We both know this is a truthful statement; otherwise, you would have little desire to read this book.

The damage done in your life could be financial, emotional, career-related, relationship-based, or even all of these things. Sitting around waiting for the other shoe to drop is pointless. You've already reached that decision somewhere in your mind, either consciously or subconsciously, which is what brought you here. That decision also indicates the desire for change.

Change. This single word, which is so complex, is the real reason you and I are spending time together. *Change.* I know you are ready for it. I know you want to jump up in the morning and rush into life to make a change that brings happiness and wealth. I also know that if we don't pay attention to what we are doing before running off into the sunset of tomorrow, those changes will come back and bite you in the posterior faster than someone can get a speeding ticket in a sports car.

Most people apply change from the stance of an emotional response. They decide to go on a diet because the skinny pants don't fit anymore, or they want to buckle down at work because they got passed over for a promotion. It might even be a decision to change spending habits because the electric company threatened to turn off the power. Any or all of them have some validity, some grounding point that sets one's feet in motion on the path of change. However, since the change is born from an emotional response, it may lack sufficient traction to take it all the way to success. Once the initial emotional response wears off, the desire to change goes out the door with it.

The real impetus behind successful change is this: understanding the *why*. When you know why you want to change, you have control of it. Why were someone bummed that the skinny pants don't fit? Why was he or she upset about not being promoted? Why was the person really distraught about the electric company calling? When we grab hold of *why* and work from that point, the emotional response becomes the fuel we need to help push us along. If we run off on an emotional crusade of change, life will be like a firecracker, small explosions and collateral damage happening in unexpected places and times.

This leads us to our very first action item, as well as your first homework break.

Homework Break

We are going to take time to find out *why* you desire change in your life. First, I want you to grab your notebook and something to write with. At the top of your sheet of paper, I want you to write WHY.

Next, I want you to take ten minutes and write down all the things that have upset you emotionally in recent times or given you pause to think about change. It does not matter how big or small the offending items are; we need to see them all in order to see the patterns that have already emerged in your life. Begin with what comes to mind first: the skinny pants didn't fit, the boss passed you over for promotion, you need to juggle bills more often than you would like, the car needs new tires, you forgot to pack lunch money for the kids, you had to pass on going to the bookstore to make sure you had gas money until payday. Everything you can think of that evoked an emotional response from you or caused you to sit and think about change in any way shape or form, write it down on the list. Go ahead and start writing, ten minutes' worth. Don't worry, I'll wait right here for you.

Did you write just a few things down, or did you find that as time went along you wrote down what seems like a bigger laundry list than you expected? Most often, people I work with (once they start writing) come up with what looks like a list that could rival the Congressional Budget in length. Don't worry about that; it's all going to prove useful in just a few minutes.

Next, we are going to begin to assess how serious these items are. On the list you created, I would like you to give each item a number between 1 and 3. A rating of "3" means it is not very serious, just something passing. A "2" indicates that it is somewhat serious and needs attention. A rating of "1" should be given to any item that is important or urgent enough to be at the top of your list. Take a few more minutes and give each item an importance factor from 1 to 3.

The next thing we are going to do with this list is to deal with only the items that are marked as a "1". On a new sheet of paper, I would like you to rewrite all of the number "1" items on it. Take your time; make sure it is legible.

When this is done, I would like you to go through this new list and pick out the top four items, placing a star next to each one. If you have fewer than four items, that's okay. However, if there are more, I want you to pick only the four items that mean the most to you. Put a star by them.

When I reach this point with most people, they have an explosively charged list of things. Those four stars seem to stick out like a sore thumb and *that is okay*. We now have four items that represent the crux of our emotional distress, our movers and shakers of the world of change. Without reliving the emotion of each of them, go back and read each item with a star by it. Look for the common theme that runs between them all, the underlying pattern that we so often overlook.

One list that sticks out in my mind is from a client who had three stars by financial items and one star linked to a lack of time in her life. The underlying pattern demonstrated that money and time were not functional in her life. The pattern showed on the financial side as money going out without having something of value coming in for it; the lack of time showed she was in need of time management techniques.

To help you look for the pattern, ask yourself this: do these starred items fall into a particular category, such as self-discipline? Personal boundaries? Time management? Relationships? Financial issues or career? Finding what general category our issues fall into will often help us see the emerging threads. Again, we're not concerned with what we are going to change, not right now. Right now, we are addressing the reasons, the *why* behind the change.

Once you can see even a small pattern to your starred items, you will be able to establish the driving emotional aspects also. Again, we do not want to dwell on the emotion, just understand where it's coming from and why. We can draw on the power of emotion later to help propel our change, but we need to eliminate its ability to jump into the driver's seat and cause accidents.

Returning to Our Lesson—Part Two

Let's take a moment and understand a basic fact: emotion can be used as a fuel to help us achieve great change in our life, but it seldom has anything to do with the real motivator that is the vehicle of change. Being upset that we don't fit into the skinny pants is all well and good, but the motivation for change is not "being upset." "Upset" burns out within a few days or weeks, at most. The motivator, however, is the real ticket to success. The motivator might be a real desire to fit into the skinny pants to look fantastic in the mirror, as well as to our significant other. A very different motivator might be getting back into the skinny pants simply because it is a requirement to keep our job. (People in the military need to remain within certain health and weight guidelines while in service; a ballerina might need to maintain a certain weight in order for her partner to safely do a lifting action.)

Being upset that the pants didn't fit served to get our attention; the real motivator is the more logical decisive reason behind the emotion.

Motivators are showing in your list right now also, lurking behind the emotion and calamities that might have happened around an event or string of events. Right now, each starred item has a story behind it, something that sparked the emotion or thought of change. Take a moment and look at them, and I am sure it will become apparent what the basic motivations are. Keep those in mind while we continue our conversation. If you need to, write down what you see on your sheets of paper, in detail if you would like. These are things you and I will come back to shortly, and the motivators are things we will use to propel your desires into the realm of real, lasting success.

This brings us to understand one basic ingredient for any recipe of success, the item that accompanies every successful outcome. That item is *consistency*. We must always apply ourselves in the same manner, the same way, the same thought pattern. We need to do this at every event that happens in life. From paying the cashier at the grocery store to talking to our boss about the upcoming raise. Without being consistent, we invite random things to happen, and sure as God made little green apples, chaos will soon sneak in and hit us like a sledgehammer.

Let me give you a few examples to help you understand the importance of consistency.

Our first example is living a life more of whim and occasional consistency. We get up in the morning, do our routine (shower, get dressed), eat something, and then begin our day. It feels like a day to go with the flow, so we begin to keep pace with traffic flowing around us. We manage to evade the speeding ticket from the policeman who nabs the guy two cars in front of us. We make a mental note to slow down a little. At work, we continue to go with the flow of the day and get most of our work done. The smaller things can be pushed into tomorrow's schedule. We pay attention to our speed on the way home as we begin to think about dinner. Since we've had the "go with the flow" mind-set most of the day, we call our spouse and see about ordering pizza for the night. They agree, it's been a long day and pizza and a side or two sound good. No food prep tonight, just light dining and an easy chair. We clean the kitchen before bed and make a mental note to take the trash out in the morning. Day completed.

Fast-forward about six months, following this routine and mind-set. Chances are good the following things have happened: we got the speeding ticket for going too quick, we fell behind in our schedule at work and had to work late three nights every week, our eating habits have slowly progressed to finding more ways to have dinner faster, cutting corners where we thought it was okay to do so. That last habit has helped us gain fifteen pounds and we wake up one morning thinking, "What the hell, my skinny pants don't fit!"

You see, even though we had some good days of consistency mixed with the not so good ones, the good days are not enough to offset the other ones. The not so good days stack up much quicker, leading our habits into a zone and area we would never have chosen in the first place. It happened more or less by default.

Now, for an example of consistency: We wake up in the morning, take a few minutes to stretch out the kinks, shower, and get dressed. While eating breakfast, we begin to think about how we want the day to progress. We also take a few minutes to throw a few items into a crock pot and place it on low to cook through the day. We do the commute to work, letting the faster traffic pass when needed, and staying within the speed limit. Since we are not spending time looking for the policeman, we have time to begin to think about the first three items we want to tackle in our day. As the day wraps up, we notice there was one extra thing that needs our attention. It will only take 15 minutes to complete. On our way out the door (twelve minutes later than normal), we call our spouse to let them know of our slight delay, and are asked to stop and pick up some fresh bread to go with the stew. Our night is relaxing, allowing us enough time to take the trash out before bed.

Once again, fast-forward six months and see what transpires. Well, we never did get the ticket because we didn't speed. Not only did we manage to keep up with our work schedule, we actually got a promotion because we have given consistent performance and displayed outstanding work ethics. (Remember, on the whole, this only took an extra twelve to fifteen minutes a day.) Because we have the desire to watch what we eat, not only did we develop the habit of early dinner preparation, but lo and behold, our skinny pants still fit! Additionally, with the raise that goes with the promotion, we've been thinking about buying another pair of skinny pants, to boot.

You see, it is so very often the small things we hit or miss that make all the difference in life. Being consistent assures we have a firm control over our life, applying the same mind-set to everything we say, do, and touch.

Consistency is also critically integral to forming good habits. Most people have heard or read that it takes twenty-one days to form a new habit. Sadly, this is not a fact backed up by research of any nature. It comes from a quote that first appeared in a book called *Psycho-Cybernetics* published in 1960 by Dr. Maxwell Maltz, a plastic surgeon. He noted that plastic surgery patients, amputees, and other patients seemed to take similar timeframes to begin to adjust. His quote: *"These, and many other commonly observed phenomena tend to show that it requires a minimum of about twenty-one days for an old mental image to dissolve and a new one to jell."* His published book went on to sell some thirty million copies, and the quote became a standard go-to item in the arsenal of many writers worldwide. Everywhere you turned, people were using the "twenty-one days to a new habit" rule. From exercise to smoking cessation, eating habits to college exam crams, the twenty-one-day rule was being thrown around everywhere.

Now comes some hard truth. The magic "twenty-one days to new habit" rule was based on nothing but an observation, not on clinical truth or practice, not on any research of any kind whatsoever. It was an observation that someone made, nothing more.

Thankfully, in 2009, in the *European Journal of Social Psychology*, Dr. Phillippa Lally published her research article entitled, "How are habits formed: Modelling habit formation in the real world." She based her research on ninety-six people over a twelve-week period. With mathematical models in a side-by-side study of what actually occurred, her findings were shocking. What she found was that the average time for people to form new habits is sixty-six days. Moreover, she found that people who performed their new habit with consistency showed a change sooner, and faster, than the median group.

Being consistent in everything you do helps form those new habits quicker, allowing new ways of thinking (which Einstein says is essential to being able to change) to emerge faster, which means you are more in control of the change taking place. Consistency enables real change to happen sooner than the norm. I hope those exciting results find a home on your new motivator list.

Summary

It's funny how time flies while you were busy turning pages, answering questions and absorbing new materials. I would almost be willing to bet that right now, at this very moment, you are already beginning to feel the seeds of your tomorrow being planted—the seeds of hope, success, and living the life you truly want to live. To think we're just getting started by laying some groundwork is exciting to me, even as I am typing this to you. I know where life can go, and to be able to help you get there, it makes all my late-night typing very worthwhile!

Right now, I want to take a few moments and conduct a conversational review of the things we've accomplished already. I'm doing so at the end of each chapter for three reasons: so that you might see how much ground we have covered, to interlace material (concepts, ideas, and lessons) from previous chapters into this one and lastly, to take a moment to reflect on what you feel and think now as compared to when you first picked this book up.

I'm going to constantly challenge your thought patterns, and continue to remind you of Einstein's theory of successful problem-solving ("We cannot solve our problems using the same thinking") until it becomes an automatic response to any challenge that presents itself.

We began this journey as we would have on any other day of our life. We picked up something to read, not sure of ourselves, our direction, or what might unfold in the pages between your hands. That's where the similarities came to an abrupt halt.

We began with finding that one of the world's most brilliant men helped me formulate the Einstein Principle (here we go again), "Problems cannot be solved by the same level of thinking that created them." Reading that, even now, seems so basically simple that it seems odd we never thought of it ourselves. However, that is why people say we need to think outside the box. We needed that simple jolt to tell our brain, "Hey, I'm tired of repeating the same things; let's try to find a fresh solution to our current issue. We might have to try something different, something we might be unsure of, but we're fed up with hitting our head against a brick wall."

From there, we began to build a framework of words and ideas, one in which we could converse without jumping to conclusions, beyond judgments or preconceived notions. We gave our conversation a little leeway in between words like *right* and *wrong*, *good* and *bad*, *possible* and *impossible*. All of those quick labels, I am very sure, helped us along the path to here and now. I've done it myself, and as soon as I realize I jumped the gun, I take a step back, and if I need to, I apologize to the person I am speaking with for jumping to a conclusion.

One of those times that sticks out in my mind was apologizing to my son Alex when he was seventeen. He had presented a philosophical theory to me which (I swear) instantly rubbed me the wrong way and I found myself saying, "Nope. You're wrong." I stopped, thought for a moment, then backed up and apologized, because the truth is, he was not wrong. What he was saying, and the premise he was expanding on, was theoretical and only pushed my buttons. However, his train of thought was very concise, relevant, and rather insightful. After I said I was sorry, we began what turned into a four hour philosophical discussion that was absolutely fabulous! However, if I had not realized my mistake of jumping the gun, it never would have happened, and what a great experience I would have missed.

Our next topic came with another simple lesson: we must always be truthful with ourselves. No hiding and no pretending we did something when we did not. We have to always be truthful with the person in the mirror. This in no way means we need to speak our thoughts out loud to another person, but it does mean *yes means yes* and *no means no*. Did that extra slice of pizza help us fit into our skinny pants? No. We don't need to beat ourselves up about it, but just being honest helps clear away a lot of the hogwash thinking. Right; it helps us go Einstein!!

From there, we had a frank conversation about change. Change needs some emotional fuel, but more than that, it needs a true catalyst. Why do you want to change? Without that truth of understanding why, change will always fall short of the final goal line. This constantly leads to anger, frustration, and a renewed sense of defeat, creating a vicious circle. This is the reason we went through the homework steps, to begin to find the true motivation for change. Doing so will help you successfully reach your goals, now and in the future. Remember those starred items, and whether they fell into categories of self, relationships, finances, or career.

Building on the catalysts, we found the underlying patterns. Motivators are the real ticket to achieving success in life. Emotion on its own will burn out and leave us stranded before we reach success. We need to understand the catalyst, motivations, and patterns to help us on the path to our dreams and goals.

Rounding out this part of our time together, we discovered the importance of being consistent. Our contrasting examples of life in six-month snapshots helped expand our view of consistent action and thought. One example returned us to what used to be (plus fifteen pounds!), the other to a new way of living that included a raise, improved fitness, and more satisfaction. We also discovered the myth of the twenty-one days to new habits. Nice thought, but it seriously lacks in functionality. New habits are formed over the average of sixty-six days. The great news is, by applying ourselves in a consistent manner, we can create successful new habits in less time.

From picking up the book to begin our conversation together until right now, we have already begun to change. You are already further ahead than most people because you have made a choice to change and are doing something positive and purposeful about it instead of simply sitting around complaining about it!

— TWO —

Let's Find Some Harmony in Life

In Chapter 1, the first part of our conversation, we got our feet wet with some new ways to look at things. Now we're going to build on that in this next part of our conversation. The primary lesson to bring forward from Chapter 1 is the importance and necessity of consistency. Being consistent will help us maintain balance as we challenge the status quo and bring some fresh, new meaning into our lives.

This part of our conversation focuses on two main topics in life: balance (or lack of it) and relationships. Each of them has significant influence on our lives, our decisions, and our thoughts. We need to begin to become crystal clear about balance and relationships in order to continue on our path of success. I'll give you fair warning, reading some of this might feel like we just jumped off the high dive into the pool. We've moved into that phase of our time together where we need to dive in, addressing aspects of life that people like to skirt around. However, you can think of it this way: we're about to go Einstein again!

There are eight main areas of our lives that are interconnected. Pushing on one aspect will affect another. Push too hard and something else is going to get bent out of shape. Neglect an area and you will see a measurable impact on other areas. Without realizing what we are doing, we address problems in our life but fail to see the positive or negative impact our response has on other parts of our life until those other parts create pain and new problems. Then we jump to fix the new problem and set off a chain of events that creates even more new problems. While we are so busy chasing our tail trying to put fires out, someone could ask us what the real problem is, and guess what? We have no idea! We could tell them it's our career, but in fact the problem in our career is, more than likely, a symptom or reflection of the real problem.

From your notebook, I would like you to take out a sheet of paper and write down the eight primary life areas as we list them here.

Homework Break—Part One

Eight Primary Areas of Life

1. *Personal Growth:* as an individual, are you continuing to grow as an adult, expanding who and what you are?

2. *Romance:* love, emotion, intimacy, partnership, and fun with your significant other.

3. *Personal Surroundings:* where you live, material possessions, a sense of order and harmony in your environment, your comfort level with where you live and what you have.

4. *Recreation:* getting out and having fun, going places, taking time to relax.

5. *Health:* all aspects of health: mental, emotional, physical, spiritual.

6. *Relationships:* family, friends, co-workers, neighbors, every person with whom you have a relationship (with the exception of your significant other, who is covered in "Romance").

7. *Career:* your profession, occupation, job, vocation, or calling.

8. *Finances:* all the aspects of your life that involve money.

I would like you to take a few moments to reflect on each area that we have listed. Think about them in terms of whether you are satisfied or not satisfied. Then rate them from 1 to 10. A rating of 1 would mean you are seriously dissatisfied with that aspect of your life; a 10 would mean it is going great and you wouldn't change it at all. Beside each of the categories on the paper, write down the numerical value you feel it warrants in your life right now, from 1 to 10, using the same rating system. Go ahead, take your time, and give it your Hamlet, "To thy own self, be true." I'll be right here when you get done.

Done? Good! Looking at your paper and the numbers you have written down, it already begins to reveal where we are experiencing issues right now, just by looking at raw numbers. One area likely has higher ratings than most, while areas some are seriously low and in need of attention. Let me be the one to tell you, for right now, that's okay. This is why you and I are spending time together here, to learn what's happening, identify what is seemingly broken, and discover how to fix it. It is also time for the first tool in our new toolbox.

Our Lesson—Part One

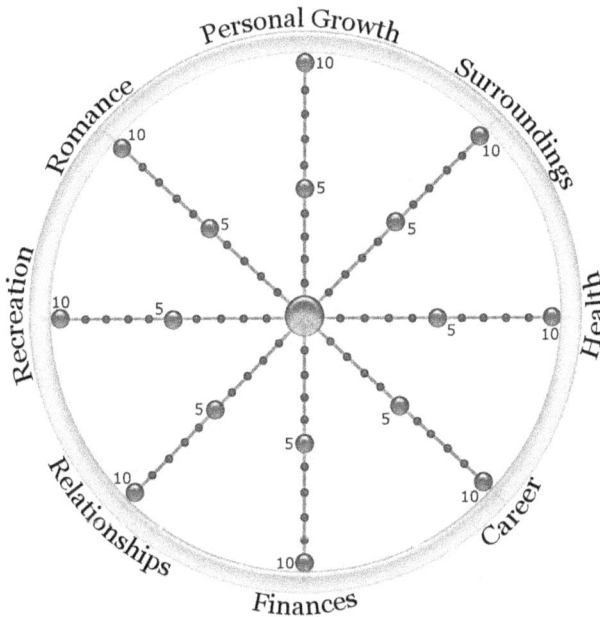

The Life Balance Wheel

This is a visual tool to help show us just how in (or out of) balance our life is. Think of an old-time wagon wheel. The center of the wheel is the hub, where everything is connected, which is also where we are. On the wheel itself, we have our eight life categories. Connecting each part of the wheel are the spokes, upon which we can place a numerical value on the level of satisfaction we feel with that area of our life. Starting at the very center of the wheel is the number 1 , the poorest of scores we can give our life. Going up the spokes represent degrees of increasing satisfaction, reaching 10 at the top of the spoke and touching the wheel. A 10 means we are very pleased with the category.

Imagine this wheel rolling along on the path of our life. If everything is in proper balance—for example, if the numbers we supplied were all 7—then there would not be any bumps or jarring sensations in life. Life would roll along nicely, smoothly. However, most people (myself included) have things going on which result in lower numbers than we would like in some areas and higher ones in others. When this happens, we certainly feel the jolt when the wheel hits a lower number due to rolling over that sore spot in life. Things roll along smoothly then, *wham*, a jolt, then smoothly again.

Also, each category is directly across the wheel from its balancing opposite in life. Romance is across the wheel from Career. If we spend way too much time in our Career, we can almost guarantee that the Romance area of our life is going to suffer. Likewise, Personal Growth is directly across from Finances. Spending too much time on Personal Growth will leave our Finances with some trouble. Each area balances, and is balanced by, another. Push too hard in one area of life and we can see where the impact is going to be felt, along with collateral lower numbers in the adjoining areas. Too much Career means Romance might go down, along with lower numbers in Personal Growth and Recreation. It really is all tied together.

Homework Break—Part Two

Now, it's time for your homework to come into play. On your homework paper, I want you to take a pencil (or whatever can be erased) and circle the number on the spoke on page 33 that corresponds to your rating for that category. Go ahead; as long as it is erasable, you're fine. (Or, you can go to my website, www.mepeterson.com, for a free downloadable PDF of this chart.)

In Personal Growth, if you wrote down a 7 on your paper, I want you to circle 7 on the spoke for Personal Growth in the book. In Career, if you wrote down a 7 then that means circle a 7 on the spoke for Career, and so on. Copy all of your numbers from your homework paper to the wheel in the book. Once you have copied all your numbers to the wheel, draw a line that connects all of your circles, like tracing dot to dot. Let's suppose it might look something like this when you are done connecting the dots:

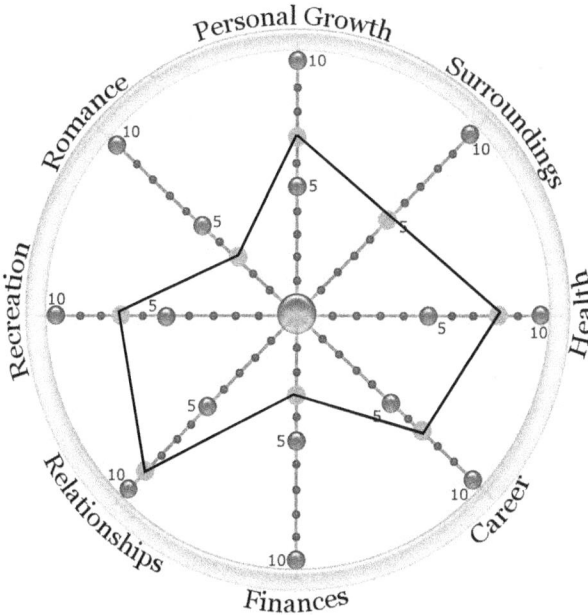

Imagine, if you would, trying to roll this wheel down the path of life. Can you imagine how many bumps we're going to experience?

Since everything is interconnected in the wheel, in the example we can see that Personal Growth is high, yet it is pulling Finances down. This would be better stated as something like this: attending our yoga class three times a week is a little more than our finances can handle right now, and causing a drain on the bank account. Also in our example, we spend so much attention and time making our Career flourish that our significant other is not being fulfilled in our Romance area of life. The example also shows that so much time is spent trying to make friends and family happy (Relationships) that our own personal surroundings (Surroundings) are starting to lack attention.

In motion, this wheel would continuously cause issues in life, no matter which direction we went. Almost every day there would be strife of one kind or another which would lead us to being upset much more often (which is why we attended yoga to begin with, to de-stress). If this wheel were to pick up speed and move faster, we would start to overcompensate in an attempt to correct the problem, and in the long run all we would accomplish would be to make things worse.

The question quickly becomes, "Okay, so how do we begin to fix the things causing issues?" Please notice I did not say, "Fix what's going wrong." Nothing wrong is happening; the example simply shows that someone is making choices without seeing the big picture impact of the action they have taken. They might very well feel compelled to spend more time with friends or family members (feeling obligated), and they made a choice to do so. They just did not have the perspective necessary to see how it was going to affect their responsibilities and obligations at home.

Here is where there is some good news. With the help of another small tool, we can begin to repair some of the issues causing bumps in life. Let's use as an example the category of Romance from our example wheel. Across from it is Career, which is doing moderately well. With some basic information, we can start the repair process. Is the person spending too much time at work? Are they giving more attention to work than to their romantic life? Or, are they actually spending the right amount of time at work to achieve a raise? We need to define what is happening in the Career area to see if we need to limit it in some way. Spending less time at work would allow us more time to spend in our romantic life. For argument's sake, let's say the latter is true: the person from our example is spending more time at work trying to earn a good review and upcoming raise. Sounds solid, feels viable and also reasonable. So we need to look elsewhere to find some support to increase our Romance side.

Since Romance is the issue we are going to work on, we need to look at the adjacent items on the wheel to find some support. You see, each item on the wheel is supported by the categories that are next to it. Romance is directly supported by Recreation as well as Personal Growth. With that comes our second smaller tool, a guiding arrow.

RELATIONSHIPS

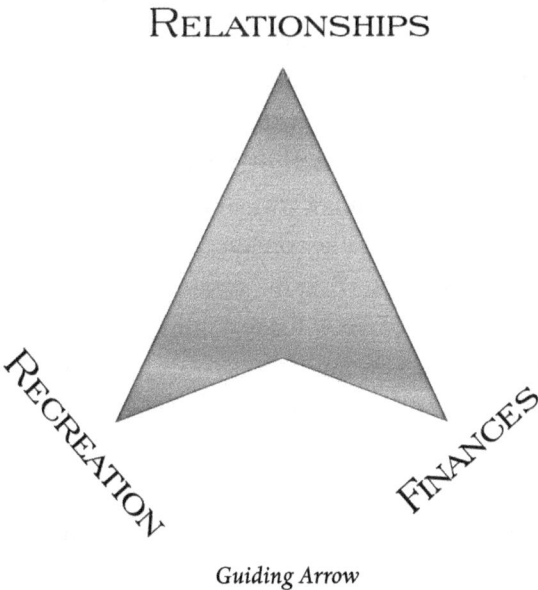

Guiding Arrow

This tool helps us understand which areas of life support the category on which we need to work. Our romantic life is given help from our recreation life as well as our personal growth. In the example, our guy (let's say it's a guy) spends a lot of time with family and friends, going out to golf or helping them work on the patio deck. He is also spending a considerable amount of time watching sports on television or working on the project car in the garage for enjoyment and personal growth. To summarize, he works hard to get the good review, then comes home and relaxes by watching sports and working on the old muscle car instead of paying attention to his significant other. Sure looks like a recipe for disaster to me.

You guessed right: we went Einstein again, didn't we? We just changed how we might look at a potential issue and romantic crisis. So, let's see if we can begin to fathom a solution for this poor guy in the example wheel.

Understanding that his romantic life is in some jeopardy, our guy can begin to change his actions. We don't want to wipe out the sports channel, because let's face it, that is something he enjoys. However, he knows he can cut his viewing time down, giving some time to the free time area. Also, looking at the slow progress of the muscle car project in the garage, he decides two things. One, spend a little less time working on it (again, cutting it out entirely will only lead to his disappointment, once again throwing him off balance), and two, when he does work on it, find a way to involve his significant other in the project. Working together on almost anything creates a better bond between people. Likewise, the free time he gained from turning the sports channel down will allow him more time to focus on romance. Over a period of time, consistently applying himself in his romantic endeavor will produce a much better situation. Remember, it took time to create the issue to begin with, so there is no magic pill to make things better. It takes work and time to fix things. If our guy's romantic life is important to him, rest assured he *will* take time to work on it.

You can use the arrow in any other area of the wheel at any time to find supporting areas of life. Simply place the area of concern at the top of the arrow and the supporting areas will be on the bottom left and right. (A free downloadable PDF of the Guiding Arrow is available on my website: www.mepeterson.com.) Likewise, any time you run into an issue happening in your life, you can take a few minutes to fill in the wheel and see where life is in (or out) of balance. Simple, yet effective, tools to help us continue our journey on the path to success.

Here is one of the main reasons I wanted to make these simple tools, to help people like "Robert" have a visual understanding of possible issues in life. Let me show you.

....

Professional Case File

* All names have been changed to protect the privacy of the client
Date: 2000
Client: Robert
Location: Tennessee

Robert is a well-groomed and well-spoken man in his mid-thirties. He works in a factory and enjoys his job. Our appointment began with Robert asking if he was going to be able to maintain his relationship with his wife as well as keep up his career. I received small snippets of Robert having a major discussion with his wife, which at first look would not have reminded me of a happy couple. However, as those little pictures kept coming, I waited for them to stop, then play again, as they usually do, like a slide show in constant repeat until I get the overall picture. The group of images together indicated that Robert would remain married for a number of years yet, and more than likely decades, further than I was being shown or could see. It also indicated that he would progress from his current position into a role of management over the course of "two seasons," which I thought meant six to eight months, but when I relayed that part of the information, Robert let me know that a season was a one-year cycle in his industry. Thus it meant two years, which was a positive piece of information for him.

There was something else that the revolving pictures indicated though, which prompted me to ask if he had difficulty in some relationships with family as well as with his health and taking "time out to play." He let me know, in no uncertain terms, that his focus was on marriage and career, and anything else I might see was of little concern to him. As calmly as I could, I let him know that unless he could get along better with his in-laws, it would tear his marriage apart. With a little coarse vocabulary, he informed me that his wife was okay with how they treated her family. I tried to relate a sense of balance to him, how they were part of an overall influence. Upset, Robert asked for a ten-minute smoke break, and I agreed. As he stood up, I could see a second man standing up with him, very dim and faded in color. My understanding was the second man was his father, trying to help Robert, and not knowing how to, even if Robert *could* hear him. When Robert returned, he was much calmer, and apologized for his language. I let him know I was not offended, only concerned. We finished our time together going over some points of balance, how energy and emotion flow from one person to the next, how they touch many things in our lives. Robert agreed to go home and "actively listen" to his wife, and see if there was something he could do to ease the relationship challenges with his in-laws.

Personal notes included:

- Robert is so consumed with making things work, he fails to see where things falls apart, or even why.

- Robert needs to find a more balanced way to deal with hostility. (Not anger management, but a personal form of release.)

- Robert is afraid of change, but loves his wife enough to try something new.

- An email from Robert's wife in the spring of 2003 related the following: "I had no idea my husband met with you a few years ago, he just told me. All I can say is thank you, because I remember that week in time. It was the first time he asked me what I thought, he really meant it, and we worked together."

This case was one of the first in which I met someone who was seriously trying hard to improve his marriage and advance in his career, but was completely out of balance in how he was trying to accomplish things. Robert is a good man driven in life to succeed where his father did not. This was the primary case that led me to make the Life Balance Wheel and Relationship Spiral, which I'll tell you about in a minute.

Our Lesson—Part Two

Since we were just speaking about a romantic relationship (Robert and his wife), it's time to really take the plunge with our next subject: relationships. What we're going to do is define relationships, place limits on them, give them a pecking order in our life (who comes first, second, and so on), and finally, show you how they interact with each other in both positive and negative ways. To accomplish this, we first need to define the types of relationships we have in our life.

To begin with, we are going to change the basic thought about the term "relationship" to let it include all the people in your life. As any relationship of friends, family, or significant other tends to blossom and grow or fade and die away, so do the other relationships in your life. Take care of them and they continue to be healthy and joyful to have in your life. Neglect them and they wither and die, often creating sorrow, strife, and turmoil.

Here is how they are defined:

Intimate Relationship
Your significant other. There is only one of these.

This is the one person who is the closest to us in our lives at this point in time. They are the ones we rely on, they are the ones we trust with our deepest secrets, and they are the one person with whom we have chosen to spend our life and time. As there is only one pinnacle to any structured item, there is only one person who has earned the role of Intimate Relationship status in our lives.

Family Relationships

Family members and in-laws.

These people are our family and extended family. We are related to them by bloodline or marriage. They are our brothers, sisters, children, in-laws, aunts, cousins, and uncles. One way or another, they are the family we have. We share many aspects of our lives with them, and they with us.

Close Relationships

Friends.

These are the people we keep in our lives but who are not a part of our family. Many of them feel like family and we treat them with the same accord, but they are not legally related to us. We share our lives with them by choice. We choose to have them around us.

Business Relationships

Co-workers and anyone associated with our career.

These are the people we work with in one fashion or another. While they might, and often do, fall into the Friends category, because we work with them, it makes the most sense to include them in the business relationship area of life. In one way or another, they will influence our career and source of income, which fits most logically with this category.

Association Relationships

Everyone else in your life.

While it might seem slightly unfair to lump so many people into one huge group, everyone else in your life is known due to an association of one kind or another: church, school, the fitness club, a friend of a friend. We know them only due to an association with something else. We may seldom interact with them, or they with us, or only at certain functions.

All of the types of relationships should be placed in order, from those closest to us (the person who has the most effect and influence in our lives) to the people on the outside, who have very little effect on our lives. Let me show you another way to look at this list. I have created a Relationship Spiral to give a visual tool for relationships.

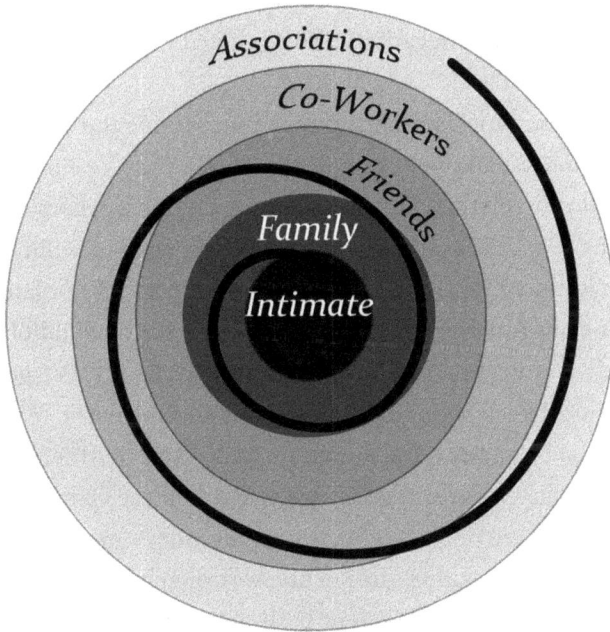

Relationship Spiral

At the very center of this spiral is our Intimate Relationship: our spouse, fiancé / fiancée, life partner, or soul mate. The first step away from our center is Family: our children, brother or sister, mother or father, aunt or uncle. Taking another step away from the center of the spiral we find our Friends. The third step, all of our co-workers. Last are all the people we associate with: fellow church members, our friendly bank teller, the local florist.

From the spiral, we can see a few things in stark clarity. If our Intimate Relationship is happy and flowing well, it spreads the feeling and positive aspects into the other relationships in our life. We try harder with family members, we enjoy our friends a little more, and we get along smoothly with our co-workers and smile at all the other people in life. On the other side of that, if we are experiencing issues with the center of our world, you can bet your bottom dollar that everyone else is going to feel it in one way or another, whether or not that is our intention. Our wife is upset; we argue a lot. Guess who is going to feel the brunt of that negativity? You guessed it, everyone else in the spiral going out.

At the same time, we need to make sure to see the whole picture here. Let's look at another example that shows the scope of how interconnected our relationships are. One of our co-workers is causing some issues for us at work. Big or small, that negative feeling is going to worm its way into our intimate relationship sooner or later. Most of the time, it's much sooner rather than later. Yet be mindful that the same issue is going to affect our friends and our family. We get snippy with our brother or mom, not taking time to explain the real issue at hand. We had a bad day and dump our plans with our friends because we're so upset. Cause and effect are at work in the spiral. A positive situation will have positive effects on everyone; a negative situation will show up in a negative form in one way or another with everyone.

Being vigilant on a consistent basis about how the negatives and positives of life move through our spiral helps keep things running smoothly. While it sounds initially cruel, recognizing—and limiting when necessary—the actual level of influence that people hold in your life can be very empowering. While a co-worker does affect your life, they do not have as much pull as your friends or family. Keeping your family in the first ring of the spiral is essential to maintaining a healthy and happy intimate relationship. Another analogy might be this: a farmer puts up fencing to keep the cattle from wandering away, right? Sure. However, that fence is there not only to protect the cattle, but to protect the adjoining pasture *from the cattle.*

Our Lesson—Critical Thinking

Becoming aware of how people impact our lives brings about the last topic we need to discuss at this point. Let's turn our attention to the outer section of the spiral, that of Associate. This is, by default, the largest group of people in our lives. It covers all of the people who are not in our lives on a daily or consistent basis. Conversely, it also is one of the most influential groups as well. All of those people represent everything outside of our home, our friends, and our family. That group contains ministers, doctors, financial advisers, school officials (if we have children), and many others. More than that—and something we often take for granted—this group directly affects our success.

Let me give you a simple example: suppose our associate list was made up of a mixture of drug dealers, criminals, shady business people, bullies, and malcontents. What's the first thing that is going to happen? Other people are going to begin to distance themselves from us, as they don't want to be around "those kind of people." The second thing that is going to happen? The overall mind-set of that associate group is going to invade the rest of our spiral. Our friends will start to wonder why we hang around with criminal elements and will opt to spend less time with us. Our family may begin to have suspicions about some of our activities (even though we might be squeaky clean) and start to form opinions based on conjecture. Being family, you know that sure as God made little green apples, they are going to say something about "those people," or worse, begin to throw accusations around of something that is untrue. Then the worst is going to happen: it will cause unwanted results in our intimate relationship. All of this, because of the simple fact of who we might associate with.

My point is this: in order to walk on our path to success, there are times when we will need to evaluate the associations we have. If they do not align with our goals and plans for the future, then they are no longer a positive influence on our well-being.

Here is an example on the positive side: suppose our associate list consists of our minister, local business owners (because we frequent their businesses), local groups who strive to better our community, and so on. Not only are we surrounding ourselves with people we respect, but we are inviting much more positive influence and energy into our lives. It will have the same cascading effect as the previous example, washing out through the spiral, bringing with it the positive thoughts and motivations of the people or groups. Not only will we benefit as individuals, our entire spiral with thrive with positive dynamics. It opens the possibilities of meeting people of like mind, which can directly help us achieve our goals.

When you begin to evaluate the people around you, ask yourself if they are going to be a help or a burden to you in life. Will they be there to add positive advice or be a constant drain of your time and emotion? Are they people who share a sense of your vision of the future or not? Do they work in harmony in your life or more often create discord?

The last few questions may very well be the most difficult to answer. There will come times when you find that people no longer walk the same path that you do, which is a good thing, as it shows everyone is on their own path to success. However, it also shows that you may need to change who you associate with from time to time. Striving for a particular goal while surrounding ourselves with people who may not be moving in the same direction will become counter-productive to our efforts.

If your goal is to become the next congressperson for your district, surrounding yourself with people who are trying to leave the area is not aligned with your interest. Instead, look for people who share your insights and passions, or people who have already achieved the same goal. Spending more time with them in our associate list is going to help us reach our goal faster.

Summary

The Life Balance Wheel, Guiding Arrow, and Relationship Spiral are all tools we can use to help create and maintain balance in our lives. Without balance, we know there are going to be problems. I am sure most of us have firsthand experience in that also, and have no desire to allow it to be a reoccurring theme. There will always be minor things happening with any category on the wheel, or in our relationships. Things will happen, none of us are perfect, and from time to time we make mistakes. However, using the tools and perspective we've discovered thus far in our conversation, we can identify and correct missteps quickly and address them before getting derailed by them.

It might take a little bit of time for you to find your own particular way to decide where the people in your life best fit, and that is okay. It may take a little time to learn to stop working so much on the project car, but as long as you are paying attention and communicating that intent, desire, and goal to your significant other, you *will* see results happen. Don't get into a self-righteous crusade trying to push people around or making million-mile leaps in an attempt to bring balance to your wheel either. Other people would not understand what you're trying to do, and it would create chaos in other aspects of your life as well.

Instead, focus on yourself and make the changes within. Change your mind-set about how you will deal with people and events. Change your perception about your finances and yoga class, realizing that the change is going to benefit you in the long run. Then start to introduce that mind-set into the world. Allow people to experience your new thoughts, feel your resolve, and see you in action. Remember, you are at the center of that wheel, and that is where the real change begins. All of your change will radiate outward to each aspect in life, creating more positive change as it goes.

For now, keep in mind that being consistent in applying change will result in new habits forming faster. Dealing with the problems in life with a consistent attitude and methodical approach will result in smoother results.

Last, be mindful of the people with whom you associate. I know it sounds like some kind of dire warning, but the consequences of choosing people who are not aligned with your goal for the future will most certainly affect your ability to successfully reach your goal. Put simply, a goal of one hundred feet will seldom be achieved by associating with people who only know how to get to thirty-five feet. Do I recommend dropping all the people in your associate list? No. Do I recommend reviewing your associates to see if they are people who have abilities to help you reach one hundred feet? By all means, yes!

Don't be afraid to change you who you "hang out" with. Go Einstein! Is this the same group of people who helped create the problems in life or not? If some of them are, do you honestly believe they are the ones to help you get further along your personal path? If they are people who have caused previous issues in your life, and have not changed, then what the hell are you doing? Waiting for them to do it again? *Really?* And to think people told me I was off my rocker for being a psychic.

When I finally took hold of the reins in my life, and changed whom I associated with, I was finally able to be myself: a husband, a father, a friend—and a guy who happens to be a psychic. Guess what happened when I changed those associations? My life became simpler, less stressful, and much happier, more fulfilling, and more rewarding. It put me squarely on the path to finding, and achieving, real wealth.

Maybe it's time for you to do the same? That choice is always up to you.

THREE

Aiming for the Bull's-Eye Because Everything Else Is Second Place

We've spoken of the power of words; we've covered some "spatial" concepts. From going Einstein by applying new thinking to old issues to determining the importance of different types of relationships, you and I have covered a lot of ground so far. What we are going to cover next is just as important, and more so in some ways. Right now, you and I are going to take time to find out exactly what you want in your life. We will do so in such a methodical fashion that there will be little room for error.

When I am working one-on-one with people, and I ask them what they want in life, I often get answers that tell me what they *don't* want. I hear, "Well, I don't want to have to worry about money." Or, "I don't want to live in a small house." Or even, "I don't want to have to wonder if my relationship is stable or not." We can scratch all that off the list right now, because neither you nor I are interested in what you *don't* want. That kind of thinking is nothing more than reinforcing a negative line of thought, and frankly, a waste of time.

Instead, we are going to focus on the positive aspect of your desire, the things you want to bring into your life. This is, after all, the main goal of our entire conversation: to help you change your life and create wealth, success, and happiness. To begin this process, we're going to separate your desires into three main categories. These are: your Title, Action Statement, and Desire. While there are many items that fall under each of these categories, we need to take the time and solidify our understanding of what each category really means. Doing so will help shape your thoughts as well as give a sense of real purpose to the actions you take. Knowing all three of them will build a solid foundation from which you make choices, and weed out distractive or destructive actions and attitudes long before they cause serious issues in your life.

Let's begin with "what" you are, your Title. This five-letter word carries so much meaning that it can (and does) make all the difference between a prince and the proverbial pauper. A title often defines not only what you do, but also who you are and where you fall into place in society's ranking system. A title of executive conjures up a particular impression in your mind, while being labeled a slacker brings a mental image that is just the opposite. Even if two titles are from the same field, such as chef versus short order cook, each conveys more than simply what you do. The title of chef has a lofty air about it, while a short order cook seems like someone who works at the local diner. Whether we like it or not, our title evokes either a positive or negative association. However, don't fool yourself into thinking it relates just to a career. How about those titles of loving spouse, father/mother, or even just friend? Sure, we might be borrowing sightlines from the Relationship Spiral, but the titles are no less important or meaningful.

When we speak of a title, not only are we referring to what you currently are, we are also looking into the future to see what you want to be. Our title has the flexibility to change when we decide it will change, transforming us from one identity to the next. As an example, you go to school, get a degree, and *shazam*, you're now an accountant. Or you fall in love, have a wedding, and presto, you went from single to married. Shaping our thoughts in order to be much more mindful of what we are (or want to be) becomes much more important when we look at the powerful impact doing so has in our life.

Next we have our Action Statement, an abbreviated way to look at what we want to do in our life. What action is going to take place as we walk our path of success? A title without action leads to an empty and hollow life. Sitting behind the desk being an executive while not doing anything in our lives will result in frustration, anger, and a lack of purpose that can lead to destructive behavior. Without action, we are left with a feeling of an empty existence, devoid of meaning and satisfaction.

People often ask, "What do you want to do?" However, the word *do* is a word that feels short in duration, transitory. Compare that to the word *action*, which speaks of something that has longevity and a sense of purpose. Sure, we could make a to *do* list, but an *action* list implies something substantial and important and gives the list a whole new meaning. An action plan to climb to the top of Mount Everest in combination with the title of executive now brings life into razor-sharp focus. That combination conveys a mental image of a person who runs a company with aspirations to conquer that world-famous mountain. With an Action Statement, we begin to tell ourselves (and the world) who we are and what our plans are. Our title becomes an asset to our action, as it is meant to be. When those two live in harmony, real accomplishment happens at every turn, every choice, and every decision.

Desire represents everything that we want in our lives: spiritual, emotional, intellectual, and material. This is an open-ended category because of all of the things we might put under this heading. If we state that our desire is to have a loving relationship with our spouse or significant other, we give our lives much more meaning. Our choices will become shaped with this desire in mind, in alignment with any actions that support our goal of a loving relationship.

Our desire, what we want to have, also changes as we experience growth and change. In the earlier part of our life, a simple desire to hold a higher paying job could very well have topped our list. As we began to experience that achievement, our desires naturally changed. They may have shifted to a desire for relationship and family, or to home ownership. Our desire is a fluid item and will change with every passing month and year. Many times in our life, trying to define exactly what we desire has been challenging, to say the least.

That, though, was yesterday's thinking. Let's shift gears and move back in time, for just a moment.

....

Professional Case File

* All names have been changed to protect the privacy of the client
Date: 1997
Client: Jean
Location: Wisconsin

Right from the time we introduced ourselves, Jean struck me as an open-minded lady. She was in her early forties, recently divorced, and no children. (I met Jean when she waited on my table at the restaurant next to the my hotel when I was traveling for business. She shared some of her story with me that day, including the fact that waitressing was her second job.) When Jean found out I was a reader, she asked if I had time that week for a reading, which I did. The first half of our time together was spent going over questions of her career and where it might lead, possible future relationship potentials, and other things. What I found interesting was that along with some answers I received to relate to her, I also got the image of a white bed sheet blowing in the wind on an old rope clothesline.

The second half of our time was spent speaking of her grandmother's house, and things she remembered from it. Three different times I had to interrupt her, telling her it seemed like her grandmother was bringing her favorite breakfast, or lunch, or something special to eat. Jean told me her grandmother would always make something good, just for her, even if dinner was something else. There were two items we discussed that were relevant to her: an antique doll and who had possession of it now, and the whereabouts of a missing bracelet from when she was younger, which I was being shown in an old purse. As I described it, she said it was her "play" purse, and that her sister had it. She would inquire about it sometime soon, when she called her sister. Jean was happy with the reading. Her questions were answered. Mine, however, were not. So I asked her, "Was there something your grandmother said, something repeated, at dinner times?" Jean was already putting her coat on, and stopped dead in her tracks. "She would always ask 'Jeannie, what do you want, dear?'" Jean started to tear up. Jean told me she now knew why she needed that reading: for that simple but profound question. She told me that for the last six months, she had no idea what she wanted, and was just living life. "Seems Grandma wants me to answer that question," she said. With that, she walked out and closed the door.

Personal notes included:

- Jean had no clue what she wanted to do in life. I would not call her lost, just directionless. Content, yet fidgety.
- To date: the only contact I had with Jean after that was in 2001, an email saying she was moving home and starting over again.

This case, while being a good reading for the client, left me with an understanding that not knowing what we truly want in life will leave us meandering around, more than likely wasting time, then becoming very upset with ourselves and, quite possibly, alienating those around us. This reading ignited my desire to begin to find a way to help people get a handle on their true desires.

Our Lesson

Today's thinking is going to be very different from yesterday's. Unlike Jean at the time of her reading, today is the day we are going to find out exactly what you want. We are going to explore each of the three topics we just listed and, when done, we will not only be able to find the top answer for each of them, but create a statement using all the answers, molded into one focused understanding. There are many people who have a basic understanding of what they want, and there are a few people who have razor-sharp ideas of one thing. However, few people I have worked with over the years have a clear understanding of all three topics at one time. When that is the case, the unfortunate downside becomes we often live fragmented lives, spending more time focusing on one area of life instead of taking a balanced approach. Too much time and energy spent finding and creating what we desire leaves the other two topics swinging in the wind, like the white bed sheet in Jean's reading. This will (once again) come back to haunt us, thus creating the vicious circle we all experience from time to time.

Homework Break—Part One

To help combat this, as well as begin our quest to find the real answers, it's time for another exercise. This exercise is broken into three parts and will take approximately thirty minutes from start to finish. You will need seven sheets of paper in all, along with your writing instrument of choice and the ability to see a clock or a way to time yourself for five minutes. What I would like you to do is take three sheets of paper. At the top of each sheet, write the name of one of our three topics: Title, Action Statement, and Desire. Go ahead and label your papers, I'll be right here.

Next, take the sheet labeled Title. I want you to take the next five minutes and write down all the things you would like to be, what title you would like to have or earn. It can be absolutely anything, nothing is too big or too small: a doctor, rocket scientist, loving spouse, bookstore owner. This list is the canvas of your future, which can hold anything your mind can imagine. Now is the time to become an artist and fill that canvas with what you want to be. Take five minutes and write them all down, big and small. Ready? Go!

The list you have created should contain things that are practical and some that seem outlandish, and that is perfect! Included in the list should be anything your mind can come up with in a five-minute brainstorming session: big, small, outlandish, funny, serious, and much more. Realizing that what is on your list is possible is paramount to your future! Anything at all is possible!

Now, I would like you to do the same thing with the other two topic papers. Take five minutes for each one of them and make your list shine! For your Action Statement, write down all the things you want to do and accomplish. Climb Mount Everest, go skydiving, swim with the dolphins—you name it and you can write it down. Show the paper all the things you want to do.

For the Desire paper, make sure to write down all the things you want in life. A huge motor home, a thirty-six-bedroom house with eleven bathrooms, a million dollars in the bank, a new house with a pool in the back yard. The biggest thing to remember is that there are no limits to your list. If you can picture it in your mind, if it becomes a thought to think of, write it down on your list. In the past, when people have shared their list with me, I've seen everything from loving relationships to books for college classes. From the ability to travel around the word to collecting tea cups for their grandmother. The list can contain anything your mind can dream of.

Take five minutes for each list. Ready? Go!

Were you able to make some decent-sized lists? Could you feel your creative freedom coming out and expressing itself? That creativity inside you is bursting with information, ready to tackle the world and give you all the drive you need to accomplish anything you set your mind to! That's the same part of you that helped fuel your imagination when you were younger, helping to create that special place to play, seeing books come to life in your mind, or even making those funny faces for friends and family. This is you, when you don't need to think about all the restrictions that the everyday world seems to place on you. This is a part of you we are going to tap to help bring some of these dreams and desires into your everyday world!

Homework Break—Part Two

So, we have these three papers full of thoughts and ideas, full of dreams and joys. How do we begin to make this our reality? We go Einstein!

The next part of our exercise will give us those tangible results we need, and the process is once again both simple and straightforward. Take a fresh sheet of paper and the list you created for your title. I would like you to take five minutes to complete this, so set your watch/timer/clock accordingly. In those five minutes, I want you to take the four most meaningful items on your list and write them on that fresh sheet of paper. Even if you have twenty things on your list, ranging from silly to practical, simple to outlandish, I want you to find the top four items that speak to you the most, have the most meaning to you right now, and write them on that new sheet of paper. Ready? Go!

What we have accomplished is this: we have taken five minutes to brainstorm thoughts, ideas, and emotions and compiled a list of all the things in your mind that you want to be. From this, we have now found the top four items that have the greatest meaning to you. In a total of ten minutes (with a few minutes thrown into the mix for having our conversation here), we have developed a list of seriously thoughtful titles you would like to acquire in life. Now we are going to find out which one means the most to you, that one thing you want to be, the title through which the world will come to know you.

To do this, on that new sheet of paper, I want you to number them (as you have them listed) from one to four. Now comes the fun, and often thoughtful, process of producing a real result. I want you to look at number one on your list and compare it to number two. Of these two items, decide which one means more to you—which one do you want to become? When you have an answer, go halfway down your page in an open spot and write down your choice, then label it with an A. Now we are going to do the same thing for number three and number four. Between them, which one holds more meaning and value to you? Which of these items would be your choice if you could only pick one of them? When you have made a decision, write it down under your other choice. This choice, between three and four, we will label B. With that, we are almost done, and I am sure you can see what is coming next.

Take a few moments and look at choice A and choice B. Of these two items, which one has the most meaning to you? Which of these two items draws your attention, your sense of being? When you decide which one comes in first place, I want you to take that answer and write it at the very top of the sheet of paper. That, my friend, is the thing that you most want to become, the one title that you most want to work on at this time in your life. This is going to become your title! In only a few minutes, with clear focus and real passion, you have taken intangible thoughts and emotions and transformed them into what you want to be! That is nothing short of awesome in action!

For the next part, we need to accomplish the same thing with the list you have for your Action Statement and Desire. Take the same amounts of time for each one, using a new clean sheet of paper for each of them. When you are finished, at the top of each paper you will have a number one choice, which we are going to put into further action in your life.

Returning to Our Lesson—Putting It All Together

Now that we have three very definitive answers in your life, we are going to string them all together, turning them into something we can very much work with, take action on and use to help make future decision and choices.

We are going to start with a fresh understanding of wording, the statement of *I am*. These are the most powerful words you can use in any statement in your life. It's not an "I think I will do…" kind of thing, which leads us into trouble. Stating, "*I am* going to …" brings thought, desire, and emotion into conjunction with one another. It tells the world (as well as the person in the mirror) that you mean business, and that nothing is going to stand in your way while you accomplish your goal. We are going to put that into practice, starting now.

Take that last clean sheet of paper you have. Start a sentence with "I am going to become ..." and write down the answer from the top of your Title paper. Make it a complete sentence. For instance, it might read, "I am going to become the owner and operator of my own bookstore." Realize you are creating your future as you write this sentence. Let it fill you with positive emotion; let that picture of you being that sentence fill your imagination, creating a picture so strong that it feels like someone has taken a picture of the future and given it to you.

Next, write the next sentence beginning with "I am going to ..." and complete the sentence with the top choice from your Action Statement paper. Again, this might look similar to "I am going to climb Mount Everest." Take a moment and again allow this statement to fill your mind's eye with a picture of what you will look like when you have reached this action. Let it become that photograph that someone has taken and brought back in time for you to look at and see, to give you proof of your action!

Lastly, write the sentence "I am thankful that I have ..." and complete the sentence with your top choice from the paper labeled Desire. It might look similar to "I am thankful that I have a four-bedroom home where my family lives, plays, and feels secure and happy." Fill it with emotion, and then let that picture settle into your mind, again as if someone has taken a picture of what will become and brought it to you here and now. Feel the comfort of that statement, the sense of accomplishment.

These three statements become your new goal in life. We are going to point all of your resources, all of your choices, all of your passion toward bringing those things into being. Given the statement *I am* adds the focus your subconscious mind needs to turn around and get in line with your thoughts and desires. This new goal, all three statements, form *one* you! They cover almost every aspect of your life, and they clear away the clutter of mundane actions and thoughts. This goal gives you the platform you so richly deserve against which to compare all choices, decisions, and actions. You now have the grand prize in sight! When out shopping and faced with a decision that is troublesome, stop and think of *I am*. Will that choice lead you closer to your goal of who you are? If not, it might be clear it is a waste of time, effort, or money. Every single thing you do, from this point in time forward, can now be measured to add to your success! Every choice can be seen side by side with your statements of *I am*. If the choice does not take you a step forward toward your goal, is it really worth doing? Every decision you make when compared to *I am*, will it help or hinder your progress to success?

Trust me, I'm not going to begin to promise instant, gold-plated success. What I am offering is a way to see what you truly want, make sound judgments in your choice and decision-making process, and begin to see tangible results in your life. In the chapters to come, you and I will take these statements of *I am* and apply more ways to create the life you want. What you have created at this point is so seriously outstanding that it almost defies definition.

Summary

Take a moment and think about what you felt like when you first picked up this book. What were your thoughts about life a year from now? Now take a solid look at where you stand, right now, at this very moment. You have a new understanding of balance in life, a refined sense of your relationships and their role in your life, and now you have been able to define exactly what you want and desire in life. The actions you have taken now set you apart from most of the rest of humanity in that you have clarity and are willing to step forward to bring your vision of the future into reality. Most people can't say the same thing. Rather, they sit on the sofa or lazy chair complaining that life is unfair and they can't understand why life has to constantly work against them. They have no clue that what they say and think undermines what they claim they desire or the actions they plan to take; they just want to complain about it. I'm sure you and I both know someone who fits that description, and here is another helpful tool in your thought process: be thankful you know that person! That's right, give thanks that you know that person, have heard them complain, watched them throw tantrums about life. Why? Because of them, you now have a model of what you do *not* want to become or emulate. Now that you have witnessed self-defeating behavior in action, you have the knowledge of what it looks like and what it does to one's dreams and goals—so you can steer clear of it at all costs! So, be thankful you know that person, because they will help you so much in life!

Getting back to our conversation, we spent some amazing time together in this chapter. Learning the three topics in life—Title, Action Statement, and Desire—and then being able to make clear-cut choices on what we want for each of them, that is amazing! Coupling that with the preface of *I am* (two of the most powerful words known to humanity), you are telling everything on the planet of your intention and upcoming actions. It galvanizes you, your mind, your subconscious, your emotions, and the very fabric of your body. It directs all of that to begin focusing on new ways to reach the goals you are setting.

Take a look at your statements again. I know you can feel the passion rising in you when you read them. That is because you have taken everything, from simple or silly to complex and serious, thrown them all into one big pile, sorted through them to find four dreams that resonated the most, and then focused all of who you are into picking the most meaningful of them. Not just once, not just twice, but three times you were able to do this. The result is a group of statements that reflect who you will become, what you will do, and what you dearly desire in life. These are things you are proud of, and can show to anyone willing to look or listen to you. These three synergistic elements are going to join together to become the most motivating and powerful goal in your life!

Want to know something funny? If you think about it for a second, you also have the second most important thing in your life already listed: that letter B statement. Let's say, for grins and giggles, that you accomplish part of your goal sooner than you thought or way ahead of schedule. All you need to do is go back to the list you created and *wham*, there is an automatic goal for you to accomplish next! Neat how that happens, isn't it?

On a more serious note, though, what we have done is given you a way to determine who you want to become, what you want to do, and what you desire in life. These are, beyond a doubt, the three most important functions to living. They define who we are, how we behave, how people view us, how they react to us, and how we interact with the world. The Title, Action Statement, and Desire form the foundation we are going to build upon for the rest of our time together in this book. As we go along, and you begin to change who you are, feel free to come back and complete this exercise again, at any time. Always be ready to take the time to re-focus to reach out and grab hold of the future. Always be sure of what you are becoming. Walking with certainty into your tomorrow allows you to deal with any person, situation, or decision with strength and confidence. Being able to do that, my friend, is worth its weight in gold.

—— FOUR ——

Supporting Your Goal from the Ground Up

You and I have covered so much ground already, creating momentum to begin to flesh out your future and bring it all into reality. To have a new goal that consists of three parts melding into one new you brings us to the next point in our conversation. This portion of time is going to be devoted to understanding how all of your life is either working for or against the attainment of your goal, and how we can use that knowledge to bring about dramatic, positive change in your life.

Remember those square wooden blocks with letters and numbers we used to play with as kids? Some of us might even have purchased those blocks for our children. Invariably, we used to stack them up, one on top of the other, and see just how high a tower we could make before gravity took over and the whole thing came toppling down. Well, believe it or not, life is very much the same way. We have six distinct "blocks" in our lives that are stacked one on top of the next, and each depending on the placement and balance of the one under it, as well as the one on top of it. The crown jewel, our goal, is sitting on the very top of that pillar, hanging on to all the motion and balance we have (or not) in life. Our goal rests on top of those blocks, and if they are not aligned well, or not sitting squarely on top of each other, the block tower will come crashing down in turmoil and ruin. Our job now is to make sure we understand what those six blocks in life are, how they align with each other, and how we can keep balance, all in order to achieve our goal and not experience disaster along the way.

To help illustrate this concept, I have created the Support Pillar.

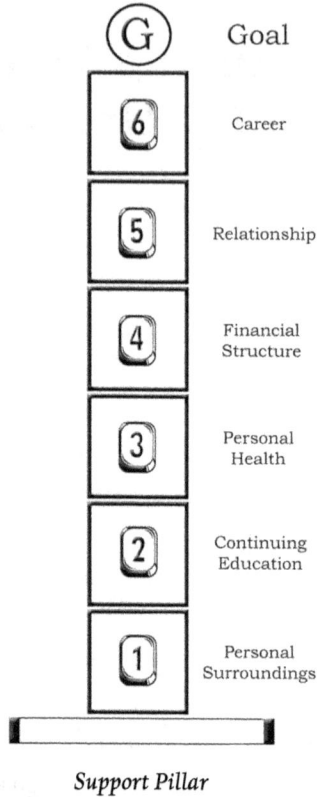

Support Pillar

At the very bottom of this pillar is you, the base, where everything in life begins and flourishes. All choices, decisions, and actions in every faction of your life begin inside you as a thought or an emotion. We are going to stack life up from that point, and show exactly why our goal is on top of the pillar. Each block has a number which represents not only how close to you it is, but also how easy it is to move or control. The higher the number, the farther away, the more difficult or complex the item is to work with. It also shows the interdependency of each item. If numbers 1 and 3 are out of alignment, numbers 4, 5, and 6 will not have an easy time supporting our goal. If number 4 is really in trouble and way out in left field, numbers 5 and 6 are going to fall, and so will our goal. We can see that each of them depend on the other, and all of them need to be stacked just right to bring our goal to fruition, yet somehow we often seem to overlook those simple facts. If the pillar falls, and we're lucky enough, we might be able to salvage our goals from complete ruin. If we're not so lucky (and make seriously poor choices), we might look more like Stacey's boyfriend.

....

Professional Case File
* *All names have been changed to protect the privacy of the client*
Date: 1999
Client: Stacey
Location: California

From the moment I sat down with Stacey for her reading in an empty conference room, all I could feel was a constant breeze hitting me in the face. There was no smell, nothing to give me any additional insight, just a constant summer breeze that comes and goes. Looking back, it made me apprehensive, without understanding why.

Stacey began asking me about her career, what would happen if she decided to change it to something else. Information I received to pass along to her indicated that her job was solid enough where she was, yet she would feel much more fulfilled if she changed careers, even though it seemed like it would take almost a year to feel that comfort.

She then asked if I saw her relocating. I opened my mouth to answer and got hit with a wave of nausea and a feeling of being absolutely drunk. I remember my next few words to her coming out in a slur, and her face losing its color, going very white, very quickly. I held up my hand and stopped for a minute, taking a good long drink from the bottle of water I brought with me. That helped me clear the drunk and sick feeling I had. I told Stacey I knew she was not a drinker, and she admitted it was something that made her ill. She told me that her boyfriend, however, was constantly drinking lately. She asked me to repeat what I had answered her with, as she could not understand what I said. I repeated myself, saying what I was seeing was her moving, but it felt like a distance away, and had something to do with a maple tree. She laughed at that, saying that maple wasn't a tree, but the name of the street where she lived in Virginia when she was growing up, and where she was considering moving back to.

Stacey asked if I had spoken to her co-workers about her boyfriend, which I had not, telling her the people I had spoken with since my arrival for work. She had a nervous laugh, telling me that for a moment there I sounded a little like her boyfriend when he was drunk. She also related that even after several arguments, all he wanted to do was party and go out with his friends. This led to his being fired from one job, and he was close to it again.

We spent the remainder of her reading time going through some minor steps on how she should best deal with being an empath (as it was giving her some anxiety), what books I might recommend to her, and other small things. When her reading was over and she had gone, I went to the men's room and washed my face. I still felt like the morning after an all-night drinking binge.

Personal notes included:

- Stacey left me a note the day of my departure. She had turned in her notice at work, and her father and brother were coming to help her move. Her boyfriend was arrested the night of her reading for DUI and possession of narcotics, and while he was in jail, she was going home.

She hoped to catch up with me again "someday when life was solid." Even though I have not heard from her, I am confident she made the right move, at the right time, for all the right reasons.

This case was an affirming reading for Stacey. She felt she needed to validate her feelings about moving, and found that her boyfriend's arrest on the night of her reading was a "message from Heaven" for her to go, now. For me, this was a strong indicator to find a simple method for people to see how one area of life depends on another.

Our Lesson

No matter who, or where, it all starts at Block 1, Personal Surroundings. This is our home environment, our house, along with all it contains. This is where we spend the majority of our time in life with family and friends. We eat, sleep, and play in our home. It's where we wake up and get ready for work, where we get dressed, where we discuss our bills and make our decisions. It's where our romantic life happens, where we dream of bigger and better things. It's where we entertain people as well as ourselves with movies and music that motivate and move us. It's where we have the ability to turn the world off and contemplate our navel if we want to, our fortress that holds the outside world at bay while we recuperate from the day's events.

Our home is what we are proud of (or not), our space to show off some of our prize possessions, our wall space where we hang family photos. It is the one place on earth that we leave from to go out into the world, as well as the one place we all want to return to at the end of the day to relax.

Our Personal Surroundings also include our vehicle or motorcycle, our bicycle, our lawn mower, washer and dryer, tools and wrenches, hammers and leaf blowers, bedroom furniture, living room couch, big-screen television, computers and stereos, even our cell phones. It includes every aspect of every material possession we own or call our own, even the type of toilet tissue we purchase. Take a walk through your home and everything you see is on the list of Personal Surroundings. Yes, even the paint on the wall.

Our Personal Surroundings comes at the bottom of the pillar because it is the one thing we have the most direct control over *as well as* being the primary thing that carries influence into every other aspect of our existence.

To help explain the gravity of what I am saying, let me give you a few examples. Let's start with an easy one, your kitchen. Suppose (for a moment) that it is usually a mess, with things placed haphazardly in cupboards and drawers. In this case, chances are you are not cooking as you should be, not eating as healthy as you would like. This is going to cause issues in your health, which puts your goal at risk of failure. Not eating correctly might cause weight gain, digestion issues, and who knows what else—all because the kitchen is usually a mess. Another example might be your bed. It's old and worn out, uncomfortable for the most part. Sure, you could make do with it, but let's face it, it causes a sleeping pattern that is much less than desirable. A lack of sleep over a period of time will decrease your ability to think at peak capacity, which in turn is going to directly affect your ability to perform well in your job. That in turn has a negative impact when it comes time for a raise, which in turn has more negative impact in your financial world. We both know that, in itself, a lack of sleep is one of the largest causes for disaster in life, relationships, and personal well-being. All this trouble because your bed is dilapidated and needs replacing! That one single thing might cause our world to collapse and crumble, leaving us frustrated that our goal is never completed.

Here's one more example for you. Let's supposed that our home is not something that we are proud to show off to people. It's either too cramped, too cluttered, the carpets are dirty, or the walls need painting. It could be anything. This will cause us to do what? Continuously go out to somewhere else to spend time with our friends and family. That causes us to fall behind in our daily chores of cleaning our house and getting laundry done. Now we don't have decently clean clothing to wear to work, which misrepresents us to our boss or manager as well as our co-workers. You can see where that one is going, right?

I'm stressing the importance of our Personal Surroundings so much because it is the epicenter of our personal universe. Every little thing about it has impact and ramifications throughout the rest of who we are. It *will* impact your finances, it *will impact* your love live, it *will* play a role in how people view and perceive you. This is the foundation where we will work from to achieve our goal in life. If it is not aligned in accordance with our goal, the chances for success become slim to none.

Let's say that part of your goal from the *I am* statements is to become the owner of the bookstore. Looking at your Personal Surroundings, does it currently support or detract from that goal? Is your home in alignment with becoming that bookstore owner, or is it such a mess that it is not going to support the goal?

If you answered with "Yes, it is aligned with my goal" then you are very much on the right track to accomplishment! If, however, you answered with "Well, not exactly" or anything close to it, then it becomes the first thing you need to work on. Take the time to go around your home and change what does not fit. If your bed is not allowing you to sleep well and is causing you to be tired at work, then for Pete's sake, find a way to get a new bed! If the kitchen is not conducive to creating good healthy meals, take the time to find a new way to organize it, or buy that new stove (or even a used one) that will help you have a healthier eating plan.

If you are always on the run going places with friends because your house is a disaster, guess what? Yep, take time to clean and fix it. No, I'm not talking about giving your house an entire makeover. If all you can manage for right now is to make your living room presentable for guests, then create an inviting space for them. Get a new lamp and throw rug. Cover the stains in the carpet, add some additional lighting, and make it comfortable. Your friends and family will respond very well, and be happy to be invited into your home. This will begin to limit the time you are on the run, allowing you more time at home to do more of the things you need to support your goal.

Our Personal Surroundings are the first step in determining success or failure in achieving our goals, so take the time and do all you can to help yourself take the best action possible!

The next item in the pillar is Block 2, Continuing Education. Yes, you read that correctly, and yes, I get groans and looks of "Are you kidding me?" almost every single time I bring this subject up. Continuing Education is one of the essential portions of our life. No, I'm not talking about the need to go out and sign up for thirty-six hours of college classes, nor the need to delve into so many online classes it makes your head spin and eyes sore from looking at the computer screen for hours on end. What I mean is that in order to support your dreams and achieve your goals, you will need to learn new things that are aligned with your goal. If the *I am* statement says climb Mount Everest and you are a novice in the realm of hiking and climbing, I hate to break it to you, but the chances of success are again slim to none for long-term success. In this example, you are going to need to learn more about climbing, how to survive in extreme weather and cold conditions, what equipment is going to be needed (as well as how to use it). The list might be large and complex, but you begin to see the importance of Continuing Education in conjunction with your goal.

Whatever your goal is, there is always something new to learn about it, some information that is going to offer insights and tips that help you out. This does not mean you need to sign up for some exotic class, not at all. What it does mean is that you pick up a new book, magazine, or article that is in alignment with your goal. Take time to invest in yourself with new knowledge, find an online group that shares the same interest and learn from conversations of other people. Continue to educate yourself, no matter what! I know that your current budget will allow you to find a way to do this; a new book is relatively inexpensive, but can offer information and add to your mind's picture of success! Learning is such an essential portion of achievement, why would you limit yourself by not doing it?

Now we need to look at how this stacks up in our Support Pillar. Our Continuing Education is resting right on top of our Personal Surroundings. Put simply, are your surroundings conducive to learning and able to offer you space and time to educate yourself? Or, is your place such a cluster mess that it's almost impossible to find a clear spot at the table or chair to sit in? Is it such a busy place that you're not going to find a little uninterrupted time to read that new book? If this is the case, there is little chance of success educating yourself, which is going to have a negative impact on success for your goal and *I am* statements. Find what needs to change in your Personal Surroundings to allow for Continuing Education to take place because yes, it *is* that important to you.

Building on this comes Block 3, Personal Health. This is a complex area to contemplate at times, as it deals with more than just your physical body. Your Personal Health encompasses your physical health, your emotional health, your mental health, and your spiritual health. In simple terms, your Personal Health represents you as a complete human being, in every aspect. Take a look at a recent picture of yourself. Are you physically fit? Do you look happy in the picture, or just seem like a so-so mood? Looking back in time to when that snapshot was taken, were you at peace with your personal beliefs and life's direction or were you left lacking in some way? Were you a bundle of nerves from being stressed out at work? Was your mind drawn away to worry about paying the bills?

With these simple questions, we begin to form a larger picture of why Personal Health is so important in our life as well as how it will dramatically impact (for better or worse) how we go about bringing success into our reality. If our physical health is off balance to the point that we are overweight, it is going to negatively impact the goal of climbing Mt. Everest. If our emotional health is not as stable as we would like (we find we are sad more often than not), it is going to have a negative impact on becoming the bookstore owner. If our feeling of purpose and direction is faltering, leaving us faced with bleak outcomes and the fear of passing away, the ramifications are going to be tremendous in everything we touch.

Each of these areas need to be addressed and brought into alignment with our *I am* statements. Each of them needs to have the ability to support our goals and ambitions. If there is stress in your life, pinpoint what it is, and find a way to fix it. If this requires seeking the advice of a counselor to help find the root issues of depression in life and help find resolutions for them, then do it! It doesn't mean you are broken as a human being, just the opposite! It means you are taking time to address something in your life that is potentially causing a problem and you are taking steps to be proactive and fix it. If your doctor tells you to lay off the sugar and begin a diet and exercise routine to drop thirty pounds, then find the diet program that works best for you and seek out a good personal trainer to help exercise! Likewise, if your minister is recommending that you join a discussion group to explore the meanings of a biblical chapter and verse because they believe it will help you, ask them when the next meeting takes place and be there!

Seek out the professional people you need in order to find the balance you deserve in all aspects of your health, and then follow their instructions. Treat your body, your mind, and your spirit with the respect they need and they will be there to see you at the finish line of your goals.

Once again, let's see how this sits in our Support Pillar. Diving all the way to the bottom and Block 1, ask yourself if your home and your Personal Surroundings supporting your Personal Health or not? Do you have the space to exercise? Do you have the quiet place to contemplate your life's direction or sit and unwind, letting go of the stress of the day? Is your couch comfortable enough to sit with your significant other while watching a movie, thereby increasing your happiness?

Likewise, number two comes into play in such a way that it often sneaks up on us. Do we have Continuing Education that allows for support of our Personal Health? Are we up to date on how to do proper exercise so we don't injure our body? Most people neglect education when it comes to their health, but you can now see how it stacks up and supports this aspect of life. In a different way, have we gotten the education we need to find ways to share our happiness with others? Have we learned a new way that allows us to express how grateful we are when our belief in God brings us what we need at exactly the right time? Like I said, it often sneaks up on us for something we might be taking for granted.

To add to all of this, remember: since Personal Health is Block 3 in our Support Pillar, it is often a little more difficult to grapple with and try to control. Being dependent on the first two topics, it might be slightly more complex to deal with, which is why it is always best to seek out professional advice and insights when we find an issue in our health. Always treat yourself with respect, stay aligned in health to help reach your goal, and you will create the energy and space to achieve so much more in life.

Next in the stack of our Support Pillar is Block 4, Financial Structure. This is also one of the top three subjects I have spoken about to thousands of people in the last decade. Most people have a situation in which money comes in only to find its way right back out again in the form of bills or items needed to maintain some basic standards of life. Some people have an ironic problem in which they have enough money, but are frustrated for lack of accomplishing what they believe they desire, or what they want to do. In truth, it doesn't matter if you fall on one end of the spectrum or the other, or even if you find yourself flush in the middle of it. Your Financial Structure is important to not only achieving your goal but it also supports all the other aspects in your life. It is far enough up in the stack of the Support Pillar that (at times) it may become unwieldy, causing minor imbalances to which we often overreact trying to correct before it brings what we believe will be certain doom. That overreaction, in itself, usually causes more issues. We lop off our spending habits to sock more money in the bank, and then get upset because we didn't even buy that new book we wanted, or set money aside to get the new shoes we actually do need. Instead of a knee-jerk reaction, take time to be sensible.

If this block is out of balance, take a few moments and ask: Are there enough finances to support your lifestyle? Where does the money go? Are your finances working for you (or just feeding empty holes, like a car payment that is way too much)? Does your Financial Structure currently support your *I am* statements, or is it going to need some minor adjusting? (In this, I mean to trim some of the excess spending in order to give your *I am* goals their due amount.)

This is an important block, all by itself. However, it does represent the point in the Support Pillar that is the last area where we maintain a modicum of control. Everything after this point becomes dependent on another person, or group of people, which will always invite possible adversity into the equation, potentially causing disruptions to our goal.

The underlying blocks (Personal Health, Continuing Education, and Personal Surroundings) all depend on the financial picture being healthy, or at least in balance. Financial Structure also has direct and immediate impact on the upper two blocks, as well as our goal. While the entire Support Pillar is important, this one block can cause serious issues to our entire way of life. Make sure to give it your attention, all the time. Keep your Personal Surroundings in check and make sure you are not living above your means of income. By Continuing Education, you can find ways to make your money work for you, or how to get the most bang for your buck when you make any purchase. Spend wisely when it comes to exercise equipment for Personal Health to keep your body in good physical shape. Research the best prices for a family vacation (thereby taking care of your mental and emotional health), to keep yourself in better shape to continue making positive and solid strides forward toward your goal. Be smart with your money; make it work for you and watch where it goes.

Moving up the pillar is Block 5, Relationships. This is the first part of the Support Pillar where we can only influence things, and have relinquished all form of control. It makes no difference which relationship we speak of; you can pick any (or all) of them from the Relationship Spiral we spoke of earlier: associate, friend, co-worker, family member, or (most importantly) our significant other. The closer to the center of the spiral they are, the more influence they have in our life, which also means the more influence we allow them to have in our ability to reach our goal. An associate is the one to whom we allow the least influence, but we allow our significant other to work with us hand in hand. We count on our significant other and depend on them to help us reach our goal.

A family member who is a constant thorn in our side is going to create an issue with our intimate partner, which in turn is going to put our Personal Surroundings in turmoil, which will have an impact on our Personal Health, which will eventually create an issue in our Financial Structure, which causes more issues in our relationships ... The vicious circle begins to form and *BAM!* You might as well form a conga line for revolving "problems of the week." The Relationship Spiral is important here, just as it was earlier in our conversation. If you need to, go back and look at it again.

At this juncture, it might be crystal clear why we need to set boundaries in our relationships. Those relationships will impact the balance and centered structure of our Support Pillar. When we deal with other people, we need to remember that our beliefs, our desires, and our goals may *or may not* be similar in nature. Dealing with other people will always present the chance to learn something new while also presenting the chance of disharmony. If, and when, you run into a person who might cause issues, take the time to consider the amount of time and energy you are willing to invest in a resolution. The farther out the person is on the Relationship Spiral, the easier it is to distance ourselves from them. However, the closer to the center, the more diplomatic and tactful our interactions must become.

All of the relationships in our lives are formed and balanced in accordance with the blocks they are built upon in the Support Pillar. If our surroundings are not conducive to friends coming over, or our level of education is substandard and not to our liking, our health is out of balance, or our finances limit us in some way, any and all relationships will suffer. Because of that, Finances are a direct foundation for the last block in the pillar.

The top of the Support Pillar is Block 6, Career. Our Career is, by nature, the hardest item to deal with while also taking most of our time and attention. It becomes something we take pride in, something that gives us a feeling of accomplishment, supporting our lives with financial resources. Our Career often becomes the focal point for our lives, striving for a certain level of achievement, which might take years of work and planning. Our Career is directly dependent on each and every block upon which it is built. If any one block has issues and is out of balance, it will have a direct impact on our Career path.

Our Career is also often based on other people. If we work for ourselves, our Career is based upon our clients or customers. If we alienate them, our Career will suffer. If we work for a company, our Career is based upon the thoughts of our boss or manager, who has a direct say in our pay raise. Even if we were the CEO of a large company, our Career would be based on the board of directors and their assessment of whether or not we did a good job. These examples show that while Career is at the top of the Support Pillar, it is the furthest away from our Personal Surroundings, meaning we have little to no control over it, only amounts of influence.

At the same time, while we often form friendships with our colleagues and co-workers, either due to them going through the same strife and struggles we are or because they are people we wish to emulate, we need to be conscious of how each of them will affect our ability to reach our goal. Many times I work with people who become mired in what they do because of friendships, not wanting to alienate that person, or not wanting to "leave them behind" while they reach for success and move up the ladder. True friendship will follow you, support you, and work with you.

One thing to keep in mind: if the *I am* statements you have come up with require a change in Career or vocation, realize the work you do right now is supporting what you will become. If a transition is in your future, begin to align your Support Pillar to reflect that new you. Educate yourself in how to make the transition as smooth and headache-free as possible, both for yourself and your current employer. Doing so will help your Personal Health (less stress, better sleep, sound mental acuity), which in turn will help your Finances and Relationships. Preparing for a change in Career should take as much time as needed, it is not something to jump into overnight. Sudden changes in any direction will rattle your entire life.

Last, while your Career is an outstanding reflection of who you are (what you have made, what you have become, what you have attained), it is not the be-all and end-all of your Support Pillar. Sitting on top of this is your goal, your *I am*. In your life, that goal will change from time to time. The object of your Career is to help support your goal, to reach the top! Remember the age-old axiom of "Work to live, not live to work" because, like it or not, we will reach a time in life called retirement, when we relinquish our Career. This should be a time when we have achieved all of our Career goals, no matter how much they may have fluctuated over the years. At that time, our Career will come to a natural close. Try to keep that in mind from time to time, if only to reflect on and create a measuring point in life.

Continuing Our Lesson

The Support Pillar is a simple tool we can use to make sure that multiple aspects of our lives are aligned with our goal, our *I am* statements. Each of them is interdependent on the other. Not only do they build one upon another, they also have an impact on the lower blocks. What happens in one section of life is felt in almost every other aspect of life. The further out of balance an area is, the more impact it is going to have on not only what is above it (what it is supporting) but what it rests on.

If something negative happens in our Personal Health area, not only is it going to cause issues in our Financial Structure, but it will also continue its way up through our Relationships and into our Career. Because the Personal Health block is so far out of line (in the example pictured below), our Pillar is in jeopardy of collapse, a cascading effect that will also have a serious negative impact on our Personal Surroundings and Continuing Education.

An example would be a man who neglects his physical health and is becoming dangerously overweight. Having done this for a number of years, he has a mild heart attack. That one instance will affect his entire Pillar in a negative way, until such time as he rectifies the issue and restores balance to his life.

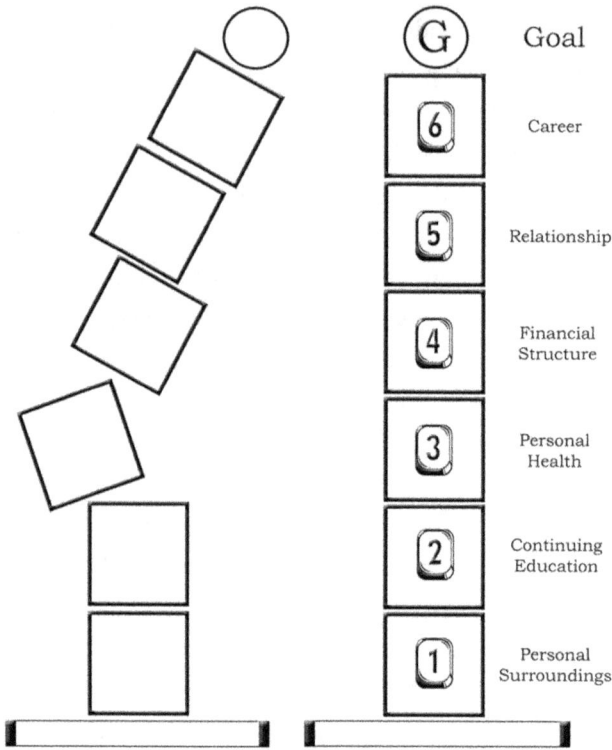

On the other end of the spectrum, let's say that a woman finishes her fourth year of college, obtaining a bachelor's degree in her chosen field. This allows the acquisition of a much better job, which will increase and solidify her Support pillar. All aspects will experience positive dynamics from her hard work, allowing her to set new and higher goals and reassess her *I am* statements.

Summary

We've taken an analytical look at life, how it stacks up for us, and why it seems to work the way it does. You and I have covered some new perspectives along the way also, seeing where things interact with each other, why one of the major life areas is just as important to our goal as another. The Support Pillar helps with that new perspective. It gives us a new way to look at the main areas of our life and helps us understand how each area supports, and is dependent on, the others. To drive the point home, let's grab an example and walk all the way through it.

Once we have formulated our *I am* statements and set our goals, we need to take the time to make sure the rest of our life is attuned to support that goal. As we have discussed, it all begins with what we call home—that place where we spend our off hours and live our life. Our home is the base of who we are (right now) as well as representing who we are striving to become, and it needs to reflect the new goals we are setting in place. I'm not telling you to rush out and spend lots of money to get all new things. Far from it. If you think about it, that would put your Financial Structure at great risk of faltering, which we can see would have very adverse and negative effects on our goal. If our goal is to own the bookstore and climb the mountain, our home needs to reflect and support those goals. If our *I am* means we are looking for a new significant other in our life, then our home needs to not only reflect who we are, it also needs to be open and inviting for new people to walk in and feel at home. At the same time, it needs to begin to reflect that new person in our life. No matter what, our home, our Personal Surroundings needs to reflect not only who we are, but who we will be when we reach our goals.

Likewise, we now know we need to educate ourselves and learn new things in order to have goal success. If we don't take some classes to learn how to use climbing gear, or take time to learn about different genres in books and the current market for each of them, we are not aligning our lives to get to our goal. If we don't take the time to educate ourselves in current dating situations, are we presenting ourselves well, or will that significant other see us as out of touch with the real world?

Climbing that mountain is going to take physical strength, mental discipline, and emotional stability. Are we taking the time to get our Personal Health in order so we can make our *I am* a reality, or are we too busy taking time to go out and party all the time? If it's the latter, we now know for certain we are going to have some serious issues coming our way. For a significant other, are we ready in our thoughts (our mind, the way we think) to allow room for someone else to help us make decisions, or are we so used to being a dictatorial person (since there was only one person making choices) that we forgot how to listen to persuasive thoughts or another person? Are we emotionally ready to be the new bookstore owner, needing to deal with clients from all walks of life? From customers who are happy to be there and see what you have to offer to those poor few who complain because you might not have the newest edition to a certain series that they want?

Are we taking time to address each section of our Personal Health to make sure we are showing the world (and ourselves) that we are not only ready for our goals, but we mean serious business in attainting them?

The same is said for our finances, when we reach that block in our life. Once we have our new goals firmly in place and we take stock of our Financial Structure, is it aligned with those goals, or does it need some work to get it into shape? Are we spending too much in outgoing bills, some of which are unnecessary? Do we need to set aside a slight amount of cash each month to make sure we can afford a list of books we need for our education? Money is nothing more than a tool in life, and needs to be viewed that way. It has no value outside of the ability to purchase things. Sure, you might feel secure knowing you have four bazillion dollars in the bank, but you honestly only feel secure because you know if something bad happens, you have the money to replace whatever broke down, failed, or caught fire. Take the time to look and see, is your Financial Structure working for you or not? If not, then you need to realign it so it begins to support your goal.

Our Relationship area of life is going to be a constant source of movement, amusement, struggle, and love. As the Relationship Spiral shows, the closer to the center a person is, the more influence they may have in your life. I do not suggest going through life one person at a time and seeing if they fit or not. While that approach would make the most logical sense, it is also a way to twist your mind and emotions into knots trying to accomplish it. Instead, think about people as having a temperature. If their temperature is close to what you need to make life good, then things are okay. If they are running a fever and causing issues in life, what can you do that might help them cool off? If they seem to be running a negative temperature, what can you do to help them warm up? If it is going to be too much work and effort, and in the long-term, no matter what you do, it will not make much difference, then think about removing them to the next ring outward on the Relationship Spiral. Do this as often as you need, minimizing your time and use of resources the farther out they get.

Likewise, if you find an associate that is going to make a huge difference in your life and will add a net benefit to both of you, then start applying more time and effort with that person. I know that this approach may sound cold. However, it will minimize your investment of time and energy into relationships that do not make your life happier and more meaningful. It will also lessen the times in which "blow-ups" happen, and those are times we need less of. Also, applying yourself to the positive and meaningful relationships in your life will also help you become very focused on your goals. Surrounding yourself with people of like minds and goals helps both of you in the long run. Remember also that we can only influence people, not control them. The only control we have with another person is how much they are in our life, if at all.

Our Career now becomes the top block to work with. Once again, it could be something into which you are investing massive amounts of time, education, and money. If you own a small business, then you are more than likely investing your heart and soul into your work. Ask yourself; does it support your goal? Does it support your *I am*? In the same fashion, being an employee could very well be your Career path, ending in what you hope to be as an upper-level executive, perhaps a vice president or higher. If that is the case, is that line of work supporting your goal? If the current Career path is going to be a dead end, and you know it, then use it to transition into a job that shows support for your goal. Find the best way to move from one job to the next, not just waking up one morning and saying, "Forget this, I quit!" as that statement will reverberate up and down your Support Pillar, shaking everything up. Why create that kind of disturbance when a smooth transition will signify who you are much better? The age-old axiom of "Work to live, not live to work" will remain true until you find your real passion in life. Once you find that passion, and you do it as your Career, then it is no longer work. At that point, work becomes an extension of who you are, an exciting way to do what you love to do. Then, and only then, is it okay to "Live to work."

Everything we have listed here needs to be aligned to support and facilitate our goal, to help us walk into our future with certainty. If we do anything less, we are going to be walking backward into our future, causing issues and stumbling all the way. Our relationships, career, health, and finances might become so damaged that they take months to repair, which will cause us to focus so much on damage control that we lose sight of our goal.

Take the time to reflect on your life, as it is at this time. Don't judge yourself, or your situations in life. Don't look harshly on any part of it. Simply take a look at it, like you were looking at a shelf of books. Are things in order to support your goal? If you run into an area in which the answer is "No, it does not," realize a few very important things. First, what has happened has brought you to this moment in time, shaping who you are in the process. Second, if something is not working for you in your life, you have the ability to make a new choice at any time. Third, your past does *not* dictate who you will become. When you find yourself asking, "Does this help me to achieve my goal?" and the answer is no, take time to address it and see if it's time to make some changes. Take the time and *Go Einstein!*

Section Two

FIVE

Stepping-stones
and Sir Isaac Newton

You and I are now at the point at which my desire to have our conversation actually started: how to transform our goals and desires into real, tangible results in everyday life. This is the point where I began all my writings, all my thoughts. My desire is simple: to show people how to achieve anything they set their mind to, to create such a happy, meaningful, and wealthy life that other people would ask them how they did it. It's also where a great deal of frustration started, as I found that people had serious difficulty in deciding what they wanted and what they truly desired. It was so much easier for people to tell me all the things they *didn't* want rather than what they *did* want. When we would finally work past that hurdle, most people had a difficult time trying to describe what they wanted, often lacking a clear vision of who they wanted to become, let alone *how* to do it.

Our conversation so far, along with all the work, ideas, statements, and goals you have made, has focused on how to avoid the pitfalls most people make in bringing their dreams to life. What you have now (and what most people lack) is this: clarity, purpose, ambition, drive, and a core desire to succeed. If any one of these were lacking, success would be moderate, and would most likely remain unfulfilled in your life.

Now you and I going to take your goals, your statements of *I am*, and begin a process to manifest them in your life. The process consists of three parts:

1. Reaching your goal by creating more goals—with a little help from Sir Isaac Newton!

2. Using imagery and visualization in conjunction with magnetism.

3. Understanding the Big Bang, the Atom, You, and Thought.

If these processes sound or look strange to you, don't worry, you're in good company with most other people at this stage of our conversation. Each of the things we are going to cover is a step along the way to success. Each of them is integral to reaching your goals; each of them infused with logic and a good dose of common sense. We are going to work with the mundane world around us, the things we see and interact with every day, in order to bring our dreams to fruition.

The first step in this is to become grounded in the thought that to reach our big goals, we need to create smaller goals as stepping-stones to get there. Ask any successful person and they will tell you to pay attention to the little things, the details. Trying to jump straight up to our goal is going to cause frustration and anger, with little to no results that we would like. Instead, we're going to take time and create some steps (like stairs) to reach our goals. In our case, we are going to fill in the space between here and our goals, and we're going to achieve that by paying attention to the details.

I'm going to give you an example, one that you might laugh at or one that most people do so often they believe it is easy. That example is going grocery shopping. Yep, we need to look at that weekly chore we all do. For some, it's a massive pain in the butt, while for others it seems like an art form with books full of coupons, recipes, and a sense of adventure. Either way, it is more than likely that this is an event that has taken place countless times in your life, and will take place countless more times too.

Would it surprise you if I said there are seven very distinct steps that need to take place in this very ordinary event? Would it surprise you further to see that if you miss a single one of them, the goal of getting groceries into the home would fail?

This is what I mean by paying attention to the small details, the stepping-stones. Let's take a much closer look at our weekly event. As we examine the process, we see that it is a complex choreographed series of steps, yet we seldom think about them.

It all begins with making that list of things we need to purchase. We've taken the time to decide if we have enough bread, not enough butter, a need for pancake mix. It continues through an inventory of the kitchen supplies, housecleaning supplies, laundry supplies, and whatever else we need to pick up while at the store. Our list is sometimes very short and sweet and yet at other times we wonder how it can be so long. We go through it, check it, and make additions if needed. Our first step is now completed, and we move to the next one.

The second step is to decide if we have enough money to get everything on the list. We've all been there from time to time, and personally, I remember those times myself. If something happened during the week, say, I had to repair a flat tire on the car only to find the tire was shot, well, there went some of my budget for the week. Finding funds a little short, I had to revisit the grocery list, take out the things that would be nice to have but not necessary, and finish the list. Then I knew there was enough money. Review your budget, and the second step to reaching our goal is now complete.

On to the third step, which might sound odd, but seriously, we need to make sure we are properly dressed, even if it means jeans and a T-shirt. There's always that question of, "What happens if I run into someone I know?" Do we really want to arrive at the store in our boxer shorts, worn-out tank top, and fuzzy slippers? Someone else might decide to do that, but it sure as hell won't be me. Jeans and a T-shirt it is, and sneakers. Third step accomplished.

The fourth step sounds just as ludicrous, but do we have enough gas in the car to get there and back, or do we need to stop and fill up first? (I don't know about you, but running out of gas on a hot summer day, with groceries in the trunk, has never been on my bucket list.) We check the gas gauge, and sure enough, we have more than enough fuel. Fourth step accomplished.

Next, we drive to the store. Again, while it is an everyday event to many people—it becomes part of a routine, something we do without realizing the complexities. It is a big deal. Take a moment and harken back to yesteryear when we first got behind the wheel of a moving vehicle, and we were in charge. Gear shift, gas, brakes, mirrors, oncoming traffic, stop signs, stop lights, turn signals, maintaining your lane, speed limit changes. By the time we had driven for twenty minutes, we were a white-knuckled sweaty mess. Has it become easier since then? Sure. However, it has not become less complex, not by a long shot. Driving is still as complex and potentially dangerous as it has always been. Oh! Remember trying to park the car in those two lines for the first time? So worried we were going to scratch the paint on the car, while whoever was instructing us was more worried about dents and fenders. The difficulty of parking a vehicle didn't change, we just became more proficient at it. So we wheeled the car in and parked it. Step five gets checked off as accomplished.

Now comes one of the most difficult parts of grocery shopping: sticking to our list and avoiding those darn impulse items. We know the store so well that we plan our cart route through it for maximum efficiency. We wheel our cart around the store, staying focused on our list, but watchful for one of those pleasant surprises, like toilet paper being on sale, buy one get one free. Bonus! We might just stay on budget yet! We finish up, minus the few items like the last box of tissues that looks mangled and the head of lettuce that didn't look so fresh. Through the checkout under budget, pack the trunk, and step six is finished.

The last real step is to safely navigate our way back home. Barring any accidents step seven is finished, and as soon as we unpack the groceries and put them away in their somewhat assigned spots, we can say our goal of grocery shopping is now complete.

That was a serious amount of planning, setting, and achieving smaller steps, just to accomplish our goal. There were actually seven steps in that event. Yet we did it with relative ease, didn't we? So much so that what I just put in the example seems funny when it's all written out, right? Yet it's actually what happened.

The stepping-stones are all of those little things we do in order to make sure we reach our goal. If any one of the seven steps in our shopping trip had not gotten done, any single one of them, we would not have accomplished our goal. It could have been that we did not have enough money, we were improperly dressed and were asked to leave, we ran out of gas or even that we had an accident on the way there or home. If these had happened, our goal would have fallen flat. If you think about it, the little things are what help us succeed.

What we need to do is take this concept of stepping-stones and apply it to the goals set in the *I am* statements, which forms our goal on the top of the Support Pillar. We need to take a little time and see what smaller goals need to be tackled to help us along while we strive to reach the big goal in our life. By setting up a list of those smaller goals, we add perspective that allows us a much more positive understanding of the path to a successful outcome. Checking off each step in our grocery store adventure allows us to see we are not only getting things done, but we are moving closer to achieving our big goal. We need to do the very same thing with regard to our *I am* statements and our goals.

Professional Case File
* All names have been changed to protect the privacy of the client
Date: 2001
Client: Wendy
Location: Oxford, England

I was in England, United Kingdom, for work for two weeks. Wendy had found me through a mutual friend with whom I was working. From the first minute to almost the last of our session, Wendy was a dynamo of energy, asking many questions that spanned almost every known topic that any person might ask about: career, finances, romance, relationships, education, family, friends, the spiritual side of life. It was a joy to cover so much ground and be able to deliver so much information to her.

However, halfway through our hour, a look of frustration appeared on Wendy's face that grew by the minute. I paused and asked her about it. "I'm missing something," she said. "I've asked all the questions I could think of, and then some, but it just feels like I'm missing something." She looked right at me, "What am I missing?"

I paused to look at all the little pictures that began flashing through my mind. All of them spoke of a busy lady; all of them spoke of several projects happening at once. After a moment, I realized what was missing. "With everything you have going on, you haven't finished any major goals you set for yourself, have you?" She thought about that, then laughed and said she had not.

Her reply set off the alarm bells in my mind. "That's just life, I guess; stay busy and try to get things done." Her frustrated look returned, and I told her so. "I've just got so much to do, and there are days I'm just drained." At that moment, I was shown a hopscotch drawing, the one kids play on the playground. It took me a moment to convey it to her, as they called hopscotch something different in the United Kingdom. I told her the point was that she needed to do one thing at a time in order to get ahead. Sometimes she could focus on two things for short durations, but like the hopping game, one step at a time, or she would stumble and fall.

We spoke of trying to break down her main goals into things much more manageable, both in time and effort, and see if there was anything that could overlap, covering two things at one time. When we were done, the relief on her face was very evident, and I told her so. "Well, truth be told, this is the first time in a few years that I feel like I can actually get my life on track." Our session being complete, she left, smiling and saying thank you.

Personal notes included:

- Wendy is trying too hard to get too many things done at the same time. I am amazed at the devotion she has given everything up to this point, but seriously, she was going to hit burn-out.

- As intelligent as she is, I was surprised she had not taken time to break things down into smaller goals. It reminded me that being in the box makes it difficult to look outside the box for a thought or idea.

- In a note from Wendy later that year, she said she had put the "hopscotch method" to work in her life and it was working.

This was the first case that I went back to in order to look at the importance of having and setting goals. It was also the first case that sparked my understanding of how Newton's third law might be taking effect in everyone's life. More on that in a minute.

Our Lesson

Now I need to draw your attention to something that so many people either take for granted, have not yet thought of, or just plain old don't care about. This is the point where our friend Sir Isaac Newton comes into play in life. Even though the man passed away more than two hundred and eighty years ago, his legacy of physics and mathematics continues to shape our lives, even now.

You see, one part of his studies became what we call Newton's Third Law of Physics. It states that for every action, there is an equal and opposite reaction. An easy example of this law would be to think of an old time (Civil War era) cannon. When the cannon is fired, the explosive charge sends the cannon ball shooting out toward the target while at the same time the cannon is pushed backward.

With regard to the subject in our conversation, stepping-stones and goals, Newton's law takes on a different (yet very serious) role. Every time we complete a goal or stepping-stone, we are creating force in our lives, a force that leads to accomplishment. Every single little goal we reach not only brings us closer to our big goal, it moves us further away from where we used to be in life. Again, for every action, there is an equal and opposite reaction. Action: finishing the next step toward our goal. Reaction: pushing ourselves farther away from where we were.

It makes no difference to what you apply this law, it is going to work the same, every single time!

Look at buying a new car. The payment system is set up to have (let's say) forty-eight payments. Every single payment you make on that car is a step closer to owning it. I'll be the first to admit that it seems to take forever, and payment thirty-six looks and feels the same as the third payment, but it's not. Jump ahead to making the last payment, number forty-eight. As you get ready to hand the cash or check over to the bank that has the title to the vehicle, you are excited to know that you are about to own your car outright, no more payments! However, think of this: if you had not made the previous forty-seven payments, you would not be at this point right now. Every single payment along the way moved you farther away from the amount you owed and became the next step closer to owning the car. Action: car payment (money going out). Reaction: debt reduced and one step closer to owning car.

Need something closer to home? How about getting that raise at work—is that close enough? First step is to talk with our boss or manager, ask them what they would like to see accomplished in order to get that raise. They might give us four things they would like to see: show up a little early, do our best to get along with our co-workers, show a little more dedication to our job, and get our work done on time. Now we have our stepping-stones to get our raise.

First step (and action): showing up five minutes early allows us to get our day planned out and in order. The outcome is that our day runs smoother, we become more productive and our work indeed gets done on time. The reaction: smoother working days, better productivity, and work done on time.

Second step, getting along with co-workers might prove to be slightly more time-consuming, yet it may foster an environment of teamwork and camaraderie will also increase not only our personal and team productivity, but leave us with a sense of satisfaction and fulfillment as we accomplish more.

Oddly enough, just by doing the first two things on our list, we have already been showing a little more dedication to our job. Not only have we gotten more done, and on time, we have also fostered teamwork in our professional work environment. We are actually, at this point, setting ourselves up for not only a raise but also for a possible promotion.

The actions and reactions that have taken place have moved us away from feeling broke and brought us much closer to the raise. All the while we have been able to check off those small stepping-stone goals our manager had given us. Short measured goals got us closer to our desire and pushed us further away from where we were. We went Einstein thanks to Sir Isaac Newton! Now that's saying something!

Summary

We're going to have a larger wrap-up at the end of Chapter 7, in order to cover the entire process explored in Section Two all in one shot. For now, though, let's take a good, serious look at the two things we have spoken about; stepping-stones and Sir Isaac Newton.

I know that going grocery shopping is a simple task, but it was a perfect illustration of just how important setting up smaller steps and goals is when it comes to accomplishing a larger goal. It's one of those things we do so often that we forget the complex nature of what we are doing. We take it for granted—and I can tell you that taking something for granted is the quickest road to ruin.

However, what happens when we move to a much larger or grander goal in life, one of much more importance? Maybe something like building a new home?

Our smaller goals (or stepping-stones) might look like this: finding the property to build on, purchasing that property, clearing the land (as needed), building the house foundation, constructing stud walls, encasing outer walls (siding, brick, stone), putting on the roof, installation of electrical system, installation of plumbing, installing drywall, painting, doing finish work, putting cabinets in, installing carpet or tile, installing appliances, moving in, and unpacking. (I know there are mountains of items I skipped or glossed over.)

The point I am trying to make (which might seem like I am hammering a point home) is that no matter how complex the list of goals needs to be to attain our top goal on the Support Pillar, it is all made of smaller goals and steps. All we need is to compile that list of smaller goals, come up with a plan to achieve them, and then do them, one at a time. As we check more of the steps off, we measure real progress in life. One step at a time, then the next one, and then the next one, and so on until we say *Success*! It is that simple. It is that easy! Don't make a grand goal in life and then pass out because it looks too difficult. Cut it down to size, one small goal after another, and you will make it there!

Taking time to make small goals and stepping-stones in our path to our big goal results in many things. We can measure our success at any point along the way, making minor changes to how we do something or even finding a better way to accomplish our next small task.

When we add in the fundamental understanding of Sir Isaac Newton's Third Law (for every action there is an equal and opposite reaction) and how it interacts in our lives, attaining our goals becomes easier than ever before. Action: building the house foundation. Reaction: increased property value, alert the neighbors that a new home is being built, allowing next step to now take place.

Every action we take has a reaction that removes us from where we are, taking us closer to where we want to be. Goal: move one hundred feet forward. Action: take fifty steps forward. Reaction: fifty percent of distance covered. Overall effect? You are now more than halfway to your goal.

Many people take this seemingly small thought for granted; some even claim it's a bogus statement. However, Sir Isaac Newton and his Third Law will win this argument every single time. Chew on this for a moment if you would: every time you take an action to do something in your life, someone is going to react to it. If you are married and you take the time to clean the house, do the laundry, and make dinner, your spouse is going to react, almost guaranteed. Likewise, walk past an overflowing toilet and keep on walking: the reaction is not going to be pleasant, is it?

One. Small. Goal. At. A. Time.

Do it that way and there is almost nothing you cannot accomplish in life.

── SIX ──

Internal Immersive Imagery and Magnetism

In our time together thus far, we have discussed several different ways to reach our goal, from the Life Balance Wheel to the Support Pillar, a variety of simple ways to set goals, and helpful perceptions to put into use. Now we've come to one of the most important items in our toolbox—we're going to discuss Internal Immersive Imagery.

For the people who may not understand the value of this technique, you may be surprised to learn that professional tennis champion Billie Jean King used imagery in her extraordinary career, which spanned more than two decades, from 1959 to 1983. It helped her achieve a massive total of one hundred and twenty-nine career titles, including six individual number one wins at Wimbledon and four number one wins at the US Open, bringing her nearly two million dollars in winnings along the way to retirement in 1983. (That's the equivalent of more than six million dollars adjusted for inflation today.)

It's not just an American thing either. Most recently, Canadian Olympic bobsledder Lyndon Rush used imagery to help train for his event in Sochi, as did many other athletes from many other nations. Yet the tool is not limited to sports. When many actors and actresses rehearse, they use imagery to sharpen their timing and other aspects of their performance. Imagery has become such a prevalent tool that it has spawned thousands of programs to help people achieve things in life. Guided imagery has become an often-used tool to help in weight loss, smoking cessation, overcoming fears, and branching out into many other aspects of life.

Just what is imagery then? A fair question, and one we need to discuss.

Imagery is the use of the mind to vividly imagine a very specific scene, a specific series of events, or a very particular way of doing something. For an Olympic skier, it might mean creating the image in their mind of the perfect ski run. For the actor, a small movie plays out in their mind as they deliver the performance of their life. For a NASCAR driver, it may be going through a turn at the perfect angle and speed. Architects and engineers see clearly in their mind a building, or a new car design, or a robot, and use that image and every detail in it to begin designing and building those things. Each and every one of these individuals used their imagination to create very detailed images in their mind, all of them focusing on one single thing: SUCCESS!

As you might surmise, imagery is one of the most important tools we are going to use. It is going to help ignite our passion, fuel our desires, and bring our goals into reality. Let's begin to learn how.

....

Professional Case File
* *All names have been changed to protect the privacy of the client*
Date: 2009
Client: Susan
Location: Ohio

I find myself, at times, simply walking up to people in order to deliver messages to them. It had taken me a few years to learn that there is an art, of sorts, to doing this without creating a scene or (even worse) upsetting the person I need to talk to. Thankfully my friend Pat (who is also a very gifted reader) had given me some pointers in this aspect.

While attending a metaphysical group meeting, I was outside taking in some fresh air when Susan happened to walk by. As clear as if someone was standing next to me, I heard, "She doesn't see the big picture." Now, over the years, I have learned the difference between a message that is intended just for me and when spirit wants to get a message to someone else through me. This was one of those times to let someone know. I walked up to Susan, introduced myself, and let her know I was at the same meeting with her. I mentioned a few mutual friends, trying to bring her level of nervousness down from being approached by a strange man. We spoke for a minute about our mutual acquaintances, and I said, "I hope you don't mind, but I really need to pass along a message to you, if that's okay?" She looked a little dubious, but said it was all right. I then told her, verbatim, what I had heard.

I knew the next line was coming, and was prepared (somewhat) when she replied, "What big picture?"

I told her that, sometimes, we needed to close our eyes and step outside our situation and look at the things happening around us, or in other areas of life, to see how they might be different than what we believe them to be. She looked down at the ground and said, "I think I know what you mean, but I'm not good at that kind of thing. I tried hypnosis one time, and it was a train wreck, so I gave up. But thanks for the message." She went back inside.

When I returned inside, Susan was speaking with one of our mutual friends, more than likely explaining the odd occurrence outside. I walked over to one of the vendor tables that was selling books when I again heard spirit say, "The blue one there." I looked down. There, on the table, was a light blue book, something about beginning meditation practices. I bought the book, and as the meeting finished for the night, found the mutual friend, gave her the book and asked if she would give it to Susan. She smiled and said, "Yep, she could use that. She really has a

hard time picturing things in her mind sometimes." I felt a familiar click in my mind, one I have come to associate with, "Okay,
we did what we needed to do, good job."

Personal notes included:

- I seldom write these occurrences down, as they are random happenings, usually short-lived with simple messages
to give to other people. This one was written down due to
its close proximity to where I lived. A "just in case" note,
so to speak.

*This file was the first time I had thought that people might not really
understand the importance of imagery in life. It helped refine my work
in internal immersive imagery.*

Our Lesson

First, we need to understand the difference between internal imagery
and external imagery. Both have uses in life, yet only the first one is
going to do us much good.

Internal imagery is creating the image in our mind from our point
of view, as if seeing things through our eyes.

External imagery is creating an image in our mind while watching
ourselves go through the task or event, much like watching a movie.

The distinction might seem simple, but in our case, it means the
difference between success and catastrophic results. If we do nothing but use external imagery for everything we want to accomplish,
our subconscious will always create this statement: "We are watching
someone who looks like us do this. Therefore, it is not us. Therefore,
it is not happening to us; rather, it is happening to someone else." The
power of the subconscious in our lives is so pervasive that over time,
with this thought lodged in our mind, we will do things to actually
self-sabotage our goals simply because the mind says it is not happening to us.

Yes, external imagery has fantastic results in some areas in which it's applied. However, it is not the tool we need for our purpose here. What we need, and will employ, is internal imagery, always seeing through our own eyes, always feeling by touch, always hearing by sound. All of our senses will be engaged in our imagery, which is why I call it immersive. We are going to create those images we want in such detail that they look, sound, smell, and feel real. We are doing this to help train our mind, to bring our focus to bear on our goals, to create success.

Homework Break

Let's do a very simple example of internal immersive imagery. The goal is to eat an apple. We begin by finding a relaxing and quiet place to sit or recline, then close our eyes. In our mind's eye, we see the apple is sitting on the countertop in front of us, already washed. There is a paring knife right beside it. Ready?

In our mind's eye (our imagination), we begin by looking at the apple, one of those nice, large red delicious types. We reach down and pick it up, turning it over in our hands. We find it is a good firm apple, and as we turn it over, we don't see any blemishes, bruises, or those little stickers that are on them sometimes. So, we carefully set the apple down and reach over to get the small cutting board next to the knife rack. We set the cutting board down and put the apple on it, then pick up the paring knife. Being careful not to cut our fingers, we slice the apple in half. We can hear the knife cutting it, begin to smell the fragrant apple, and see some of the apple juice on the cutting board. As we finish slicing it apart, we can see the seeds in the middle of the core, and more apple juice on the cutting board. Boy, does that apple smell good! We set one half of the apple aside, and take the other section and cut it in half. The cut is just as firm as the first one we made, the knife slipping easily downward as we cut, making that *thunk* sound when the knife hits the cutting board. We pick up one quarter, and apple juice is on our fingers. The core and seeds need to come out, so we carefully slice the seeds and core material out of the apple, leaving them on the cutting board. We bring the apple quarter up to our mouth, and we can smell that delicious smell of a fresh-cut apple. We take a bite. Crunchy, sweet, and juicy, just as we thought it would be. A moment later, that slightly bittersweet taste all good apples have pervades our taste buds. Yep, this is one seriously delicious apple! Our stomach rumbles that great rumble of approval while we finish eating the rest of the apple quarter.

In our example, we engaged all of our senses: sight, touch, sound, smell, and taste. We did so just as if we were cutting the apple in real life, a simple example to expand our understanding of this unique tool. This is internal immersive imagery. What is even more impressive is the fact that you have now engaged your taste buds and your stomach into waiting for another taste of that apple. Simply thinking about this in the way you have, your body is already in a mode of reaction and anticipation!

Let's go a step further, something a little more complex. Our goal this time is to envision being on the beach by the ocean. We've already unpacked the car and are heading toward the sand.

The sun feels warm on our face; the light breeze coming up from the ocean is refreshing. We reach the sand and bend down take our sandals off, feeling a little tension ease with being barefoot. When our feet touch the sand, we immediately feel the warmth of it, yet we also feel its softness. Some of the grains of sand go in between our toes as we wiggle them, stretching them out. As we walk along, feeling the sand give way under our heels, we take note of the feeling, being so different than walking on soft grass or dry dirt, warm and soft, cushioning each step along the way. A little closer to the edge of the water looks like an excellent place to lay out our beach towel, and we head in that direction, smiling at the seagull that seems to be just lazily floating in the air.

When we reach our spot, we spread the towel out and set our sandals next to it. Then we sit down on the towel, feeling the sand sink under us. The sun and the sand have already warmed up the towel, and it feels like a warm heating pad, soft and comfortable. Looking out to the ocean, we see the waves coming in, nice regular intervals, that great soothing sound as they come washing in and then retreating, leaving the sand wet. There are a few birds out there, running in front of the waves, looking like they are trying not to get wet, yet they also seem to be chasing the water away as it recedes back in the ocean. Back and forth they go, like a comical dance, seeming to say, "Dry feet, dry feet, dry feet … now, run and chase the water, no, wait! Go back, dry feet, dry feet!" as they run in and out.

The taste of ocean salt is in the air as a light breeze flows up the beach. We close our eyes and listen to the waves coming in and out.

Again, we engaged all of our senses in this imagery, from how the wind feels to the warmth of the sand. We smelled the sea salt on the breeze coming in from the waves and watched as the seagull floated in the wind.

Using internal immersive imagery helps train our mind to focus on details, and the more real we can make that image, the more the mind will work to see it, feel it, taste it, listen to it, and smell it. Taking the time to fill in all the little details is essential to making our goals become reality, training our mind to work toward that goal. It also leads us to our next topic.

Returning to Our Lesson

While we work toward our goals in life, even the smaller ones we create, and use internal immersive imagery, we are also going to magnetize our body and mind. In effect, we are polarizing who we are, our entire being.

Think of it this way. If you take a magnet and rub it against another metal object, starting at one end and going to the other, then repeating that same process over and over, you polarize that other metal object. It will now have a positive end and a negative end.

By using internal immersive imagery, and going through the same imagery several times, we begin to polarize our lives as well as our mind. Think this might be a little far-fetched? Let's try this one on for size, then.

Our goal is to purchase a new car. We've gone to the dealership and sat in that new car, so we know how it feels, how it looks, what it smells like, what the door sounds like when closing, how quiet it is inside. We take all of that and create imagery that we use at home, replaying different scenes in our mind: going for a drive and feeling the wind with the windows rolled down, what it smells like when we stop and put gas in the car, how the seats feel while sitting at the red light on our way to work. The imagery we create is all-encompassing, using all of our senses.

One of the first goals we know we need to achieve is to have a certain amount of money in the bank. So, we start by using internal immersive imagery for this as well. We walk up to the bank teller and deposit money into our account, and we get the receipt. It shows us the amount in the account is growing larger with every deposit, taking us one step closer to owning that new car. Going through this imagery on a daily basis helps us stay focused on our larger goal, while at the same time it polarizes our thoughts, which takes form in our actions. We become magnetized to seeing the amount in the account getting larger. Someone asks if we would like to go out to eat. However, we know we did this just a few days ago, and our bank imagery jumps into our mind, and we decline. Maybe some other time.

What might have been a very typical occurrence of going out to eat with our friends all the time has become an every-now-and-again kind of thing, and truth to tell, we might not even think much of declining the offer. Why? Because our mind is focused on our imagery of the bank account getting larger, not going out to eat. We have polarized ourselves into saving money for our goal instead of spending it the way we used to. Every single time we do make the deposit in the bank, it adds belief and credibility to our imagery, which in turn fuels our desire to accomplish our goal. Nice little circle of events, wouldn't you say?

Our use of imagery has helped us condition our thoughts, our reflexes, and our responses to achieve success in our goals. Every action

we begin to take, and every reaction we have to situations, will begin to reflect our goals. In going out to eat, we might find ourselves
remembering that a coupon came in the mail for our favorite restaurant, and we use it on one of the occasions we go out with friends. Even
this shows that our mind is looking for almost any way possible to save
money for that new car!

Over a period of time, our actions and reactions will become automatic, taking us steps closer to success in our goals. We decline or
move away from spending habits that will take us further away from
the new car and begin to look for situations that help us get that next
step closer to it. All of this because we are polarizing our mind, our
thoughts, and our actions using imagery.

Summary

Internal immersive imagery is one of the strongest tools we have to
use in achieving our goals and *I am* statements. We can use it to train
our mind to focus on our goals, to train our actions and reactions (just
like professional athletes do), to rid ourselves of negative thoughts
and emotions while replacing them with positive ones. The changes
we can make in our lives by employing this dynamic tool are nothing
short of amazing!

At the same time, we are going to magnetize ourselves. Our subconscious mind, our thoughts, our emotions, our actions and reactions, all of them will begin to take on the characteristics of our goal,
to take us the next step closer to success and fulfillment.

From the previous chapter, in learning that we make smaller goals
in order to accomplish our larger ones, we begin to see how this
whole process is going to work. You create an image for your goal
and *I am* statements, while creating smaller goals and imageries to fit
them, all of this is going to begin to change who you are, what you do
as well as how you do them. Your entire being is going to be aligned
and magnetized with these goals, which means every action (and reaction) you make will be weighed in your mind. If the action or decision

brings you closer to the finish line, you'll do it. If it doesn't, you will find yourself thinking very seriously about it before you do it, and often times making judgments quickly that are aligned with where you are going.

All of this is going to be in your life with the power of your thoughts!

SEVEN

Your Thoughts, the Atom, and the Big Bang

An Open Chapter to Engage Your Mind

We've come quite a long way in our conversation, and it's time for me to give you some things to think about, to make your mind go, "Wow!" One of my final tasks for our time together is to help you see past the normal day-to-day reality of things, to look past the mundane and see grand possibility, limitless potential, and understand it hinges on you. You hold incredible power in your actions (what you do), your perceptions (how you think), and your desires (what you want). It's time to turn your mind into a *next-step* creating machine, understanding that the word *impossible* has no place in our new way of thinking.

To kick all of this off, let's return once again to our good friend Sir Isaac Newton, who, it seems, left us with yet another (of many) laws of physics. Earlier, we had spoken about his Third Law, which states that every action has an equal and opposite reaction. That law helped us understand not only that every step we take moves us forward, but also that time removes us from where we were. This next law I want to discuss is the one Newton labeled the Conservation of Energy, which basically says that energy can neither be created nor destroyed, it can only change form.

Sometimes, science classes demonstrate this law by burning a match. The explanation is that it turns into ash, releases heat and light, and creates vapor and smoke. We can account for how the energy went from being stored in the form of a match to being expressed as all those other compounds and components, showing that energy only changed form and was not destroyed, as it might seem. The first time I witnessed this, I thought about it in a scientific study kind of way, as I needed to for the upcoming exam. (If memory serves, I received a low B- for that exam, go figure.)

Yet here I am, three decades later, taking that same law and fundamental understanding and placing into a written work. Why? That would be the most obvious question, and the answer is both complex and simple.

Both the scientific and theological establishments generally agree on one very specific thing. All matter in the universe came from one point. Science calls it the Big Bang theory; theology refers to it as the moment of creation. ("Let there be light.") Each of them is referring to a single point of matter that became the universe as we know it. (The theories and beliefs of both establishments differ wildly directly after that instant.) For our conversation though, it remains one of the most relevant items due to its ability to change our understanding or our conception of energy.

All the matter, energy, light, rocks, water, dust, books, cars, planes, submarines, galaxies … everything in the universe came from that singular point. That includes you and me. At some point in time, way back when, atoms in your body were directly connected to and associated with all the other atoms in the universe. An atom in your body today might have been connected to an atom in a supernova from a galaxy on the other side of the universe. Since the average human body is made up of over seven octillion atoms (*that's a 7 with 27 zeros after it*), it is not such a mind-blowing thought that we share atoms with planets and suns in far-flung galaxies hundreds of light years away. My point is this: we are made up of the same thing as all the planets, suns, and galaxies in the universe. Go anywhere in the universe and there is a relative piece of matter. Just as a family has aunts, uncles, moms, dads, cousins, brothers, and sisters, you have a connection to practically any other spot in the universe. *You are a part of, and connected to, everything.*

If that were not enough to jolt your mind and thought into "Where does real actually begin?" then perhaps this might. Take a moment to remember a science class, that one that spoke about the makeup of an atom. The core of an atom (the nucleus) is made of protons and neutrons, while whizzing around the core are the electrons. In that atom, there is empty space between the nucleus and the electrons, right? Well, this might grab your attention: if we were to take an atom and make it bigger (just for example) and then say the nucleus of an atom was about the size of a regular marble, then an electron would be something like a small piece of dust two thousand, six hundred feet away. (That's almost a half-mile of empty space there!) What does this mean to us in the here and now? It means that even though your physical body appears to be solid, in actuality, it is 99.999% empty space.

Sticking with the concept of energy, we come to the human brain. What a lovely complex organ it is, full of neurotransmitters, synaptic nerves, and a whole host of things I can't even begin to pretend to understand. However, I do know this: everything that happens in the brain is nothing more than electrical impulses. There is nothing mechanical going on up there, no machines running like computers, no paper print-outs. It all boils down to bioelectric material running around like a giant thunderstorm in your skull. This fits into our conversation in one simple summation: you are in control of those thought processes; you control that energy.

So, I have a thought, I think about it, that energy and command is sent to my fingers and something like thirty-five muscles go into action and move to type the words I want to see on my computer screen. And that happens with *every single key stroke*! So, when you fire off that text or email, think about how much control you have over the energy it takes to do that seemingly simple task.

Professional Case File

* *All names have been changed to protect the privacy of the client*

Date: 1999

Client: Linda

Location: Winnipeg, Manitoba—Canada

On one of many trips to Canada for work, I had the opportunity to read for Linda. She had heard that sometimes a reader would like to have an item owned by a loved one in spirit if they were looking for information about, or from, that loved one. She had brought a few items of her grandmother's with her during her reading, and we made use of them.

Linda had brought a photograph taken by her grandfather when both he and her grandmother were young. When I picked it up, I was shown a cream-colored car, which had something wrong with the brake lights, and relayed this to her. She let me know that her grandmother often told the story of how they always had issues with the rear turn signals, that they would short out or something, and they would blink on their own accord. I also relayed that this vehicle had been stored, and Linda played in it as a young girl while her parents and family visited inside the house. She relayed a few small stories about the "adventures" she would take in that wonderful, worn-out old car.

The other item she brought was a pair of her grandmother's earrings. When she placed these on the palm of my hand, the images came through so quickly that I said out loud, "You need to slow down," which earned me an odd look from Linda. The speed at which the images came through did slow down, and one by one I related just the picture and the emotion attached to them. A special star on the Christmas tree, little marbles on a hardwood floor that rolled into the kitchen, a toy sailboat, an old four-poster bed (no canopy) with an odd design on the headboard. Then the images changed, with emotions of love and a feeling like an easy Sunday afternoon. I now saw a yellow lunch pail with a bunny, a flat stone by a rosebush and last, a flag displayed on a front porch (like a flag for holidays or celebrations). Linda had some tears as she relayed that each of those things were special to her and her grandmother, each had some special meaning. The last image, the flag, was in the last photo she took of her grandmother's house.

Personal notes included:

- The information Linda received was more of a confirmation that her grandmother was indeed all right. She had worried for years about that, as her grandmother had passed away in her sleep at home, and Linda always felt bad about not being there.

- The rock by the rose bush was where the two of them had buried a small pet, but it had more meaning because her grandmother took the time to explain how life's circle moved on all the time, a teaching Linda never forgot. It helped her know everything was okay.

This case file has always been important to me, as it illustrates the use of psychometry, the ability to connect with the energy of people, places, or things through touch.

Returning to Our Conversation

Just like a great late-night TV sales commercial, *Wait! There's more!*

Reading and comprehending this text is another outstanding example of something we so often take for granted, yet two startling processes are taking place. First, our eyes actually see things upside down. Our brain is the manipulator that turns images "right side up" when we "see" them. Second, by the time you read this sentence, you will be a few milliseconds in the past. Due to reflection of light, and the amount of time it takes to comprehend what we see, a very brief moment has passed, placing everything we see in the past. Take driving our car as an example; we are actually reacting to something that has already happened. Yet the astounding thing is that we react, thinking about the future, in order to have things happen in the "now." Yes, I am talking about such a miniscule amount of time that it is imperceptible, yet it remains a fact. We see in the past, we react into the future, which creates our now. Let me show you.

Let's say I drop a glass. It takes time to realize it slipped out of my hand. Then it takes time for me to think about catching it. Then it takes time to formulate an idea of catching the glass, since I have to think about the path it is taking on the way to the floor, and then I have to decide where in that path I need to put my hand. Then I have to move my body to that future point in order to catch the glass. By the time I know I have caught the glass, the event is already over due to the fact it takes my brain a split second to have my eyes tell me the glass is in my hand, as well as the nerves in my hand confirming that yes, I have the glass in my hand—all this before my brain can tell me, "Yes, we caught the glass."

I saw something in the past, I reacted into the future, and I created the now by catching the glass. If I missed, then I would be on the move to get the broom and dustpan, but that's a different story. The incredible thing here is that my body reacted on very little thought— all those muscles moving, my heart beating, blood flowing, chest breathing, and on and on. If I had to think of every single little detail of body mechanics and muscle movement to make that action happen, the glass would shatter every single time, because I would miss it, every single time.

All of these things I mention are here to show you a different aspect of thinking, a different view of the world, from how we see things to how we manipulate energy and thought to create actions. From controlling our thoughts to understanding that we are, at some very basic level, connected to everything in the universe, our thoughts impact our reality, either by action or reaction. From that point on, things will never be the same. Everything we do in life will alter what is, not only in our own world of home and family, but also in the larger world of people and things around us. You may think that your life has little impact on the world, yet because of one little physics law, every action you take will have an equal and opposite reaction. That reaction bumps into and affects someone else, thus causing them to take an action, and they cause a reaction, and so on.

Hard to fathom? How about this (an example blown way out of proportion for the sake of making a point): let's say you normally purchase a candy bar every Friday as a treat to yourself on the way home from work. Then you decide to diet for a month to drop a few pounds to fit into your swimsuit for summer, so you stop purchasing the candy bar. Action/reaction is going to have this effect: the company sells less chocolate, they purchase less cocoa from their supplier, the supplier purchases less cocoa from the exporter in Africa, the exporter purchases less of it from the farmer, the farmer cuts back how much he will harvest and must raise prices to keep his profit, he will charge the exporter more, the exporter raises prices, the supplier gets the cocoa and raises prices, the chocolate company gets the cocoa and raises prices. The next time you go to purchase that same candy bar, the price is higher. Your action to not purchase the candy bar reached halfway around the world to a little farmer in Africa, and that was just a simple thing! Still want to say our life has no impact on the rest of the world?

Multi-Chapter Wrap-Up

I would like to go back a few thousand words and reach into Chapter 5, pulling a few things out from there, then doing the same for Chapter 6 and this chapter also. We need to wrap together all the things we have spoken about in order to have a serious and comprehensive understanding of *how* we do things.

In order of appearance in our conversation, those topics are as follows:

- Every goal is the result of a series of smaller goals
- Newton's Third Law of Physics = action/reaction
- Internal immersive imagery
- Magnetism
- Newton's Conservation of Energy
- The Big Bang and creation ("Let there be light")
- Personal connection to everything
- Empty space and purposely directing thought energy

All of these topics, when placed in conjunction with one another, produce a conceptual way of how to do something that results in successful outcomes. These outcomes produce continuing momentum in accomplishing the next goal or item on the list. Let's take a look at the entire process, now that we have all the component parts.

We have a main goal, to take a cruise on an ocean liner. We know there are going to be smaller goals needed here, so let's list them. (Or, at least the major ones, as it may be going overboard to list "Bring extra toilet paper.")

Goal: Take a cruise to the Bahamas
- Find cruise dates that are compatible with your work schedule
- Find cruise options that meet your budget
- Book the cruise
- Decide whether to fly or drive to port where ship is
- Set budget for this vacation
- Save money for this vacation
- Purchase any additional clothing needed
- Pack for vacation
- Go on vacation!!

Let's start with the very first goal, to find cruise dates that are compatible with your work schedule. This smaller goal sets all of our material into motion.

1. By finding those dates that are compatible with our work schedule and responsibilities, we add excitement (emotional fuel) to the accomplishment of our goal.

2. We also evoke Newton's Third Law realizing two things: we have taken a step closer to success, which pushes us away from where we were only moments before.

3. Having those dates in mind allows us to begin to lightly daydream (a form of internal imagery) about going on vacation.

4. We also have started a process of applying polarity and magnetism to our lives. We will attract or repel ideas and future events (things) based on whether or not it helps us get to our goal.

5. We begin to realize that we are in control of what happens in our life; we are taking our thoughts and turning that energy into a future reality. The actions we are taking are going to result in a "now" moment of stepping off the cruise ship onto the beach in the Bahamas.

All of this is transpiring simply by taking that first small step on the path to achieving our main goal. Each and every successive step will only add more energy, more polarization and magnetism, and more focus to our future success.

By the time we get down the list and start working on saving money for our vacation, we have already taken the time to begin our internal immersive imagery, creating a moving image in our mind of standing on the ship as it sails along, the wind blowing through our hair, the smell of salt air, the sound of people laughing. This, in conjunction with polarity and magnetism in action in our lives and the action/reaction process, we can see that not only have we moved farther away from our old position in life (just thinking about going on vacation) but we are well along the path to success and going on that cruise! We have such a positive feeling about it that we have become almost giddy, smiling and laughing, interacting in positive and pleasant ways with many of the people around us.

Practicing our imagery on a daily basis brings more of all of this: better mood, positive people coming back to us with an enhanced mood and outlook simply because we laughed and smiled with them—now they are laughing and smiling more often and returning that energy to us. The reaction phase in our life is polarized now, bringing us more positive outlooks, situations, and outcomes. We have moved our lives from a place we were before and now have infused it with positive energy and responses.

We go clothes shopping and begin the process of packing our bags, almost bursting at the seams with excitement and positive energy knowing our goal is only hours away at this point. People are now telling us they're going to miss us for the ten days we will be gone, and they mean it!

Can you see that just by focusing our minds, our positive energy, and our actions on our smaller goals, while walking the path to achieve our larger goal, we have changed the world around us? We have created better work environments, more harmonious friendships and associations, and added positive energy and a sense of well-being to our entire lives!

When we get back from this vacation, guess what's going to happen? We are going to begin the process again by setting a new goal, one which I would almost bet is going to be bigger and grander than something we had envisioned before! All of this simply because we now have a huge understanding that yes, we can accomplish it!

Over a period of time in your life, using this type of system will have some rather dynamic and positive effects and results. After reaching goals and experiencing those positive outcomes, we are conditioning our mind and body to continue in the same manner, at every event, every conversation, every action. A result would be when a new opportunity arrives in our lives: where before we may have casually dismissed it as too big or too complex to do (*There's no way I can afford to do that!*), we will now see it as a grand opportunity to grow and accomplish greater things. (*Wow, not only can I do that, but look at all the incredible things that will happen because of it!*)

We will go from being meek and mild about change to a being someone who is actively looking for change and new adventures in everything we see, do, and touch. We will grow away from a mindset of *not enough* (not enough money, not enough love in our life, not enough ability to get a raise) and move into an understanding of the ability to create wealth in all areas of life, at any time, any day, any moment. We will understand that every thought we have, every step we take, every action we take will bring us our true desires in life.

Reaching that point only requires you to start at the beginning: set your goals, use your statements of *I am,* and add a little belief in yourself and what you do.

Think of those people who seem to have great lives, how simple it looks when they set goals and achieve them. We used to admire them, we used to get jealous of them, we had a difficult time figuring out how they made it all look so easy. Now you know how they do it, and guess what? Someday, someone is going to look at you that very same way!

If that isn't a big enough change in your life, then very honestly, I don't know what is.

EIGHT

"Everything Changes and Nothing Stands Still"—Heraclitus

Change is the only constant in the universe. That's the popular quote you've more than likely heard or read from time to time, but it stems from the Greek philosopher Heraclitus, who died in 475 B.C. From nearly 2,500 years in the past his voice rings out his warning, "Everything changes and nothing stands still." Will you heed his warning?

With the conversation you and I have had, you have the tools and information to tackle change, to turn it from challenge into success. Taking control of your life will mean having more control of the changes happening, which has an instant result of increased stability.

Yet Heraclitus still echoes in my mind, casting his warning far and wide for those who take time to hear. If you listen, ever so closely, you can almost hear him saying, "Everything changes, either by choice or by reaction. Nothing stands still, for that brings stagnation. Will you act, or react? Will you flow within your life, or will you allow yourself to become stagnant? This is the crux of the word *choice*—to decide one way or another."

Our Lesson

Our time together, through this conversation and the dialogue you've had within your own mind, has brought us directly to that point we so often try to avoid. From this point on, there is no more continuing on as things were. That would be lying to yourself, and neither of us wants to see that happen. So, from this point on, it is either turn left or turn right. There is no straight ahead. It's time for you to make a choice.

If you decide to turn left, you will continue your life, much as it was before, not applying what you have learned within the framework of this conversation we have had. Yet there will be one huge difference: you will live your life always knowing you have the ability to create success. If that becomes your choice, then I'll still respect you for it. I'll be grateful for the conversation we had, and I would leave you with a single thought: if you ever decide to make a difference in your life, just pick this book up again, open it to page one, and we can have another conversation.

If you make a choice to turn right, then it's time to grab hold of your future, and use your willpower to shape the outcome of your choices and decisions. Turning right means setting out on a new path of life, one that can result in true wealth. Turning right is a choice to change, to succeed, and to see life as a wonderful grand adventure waiting for you to set new goals and soar to new heights!

Switching Gears

Now, if you would allow me, I'd like to change focus slightly, similar to changing from the suit and polo shirt I've been wearing to a pair of jeans and a T-shirt. I'd like to go from the person who has been opening doors to new perspectives in your mind to the guy who is sitting here and typing along. I'd like to take just the last little bit of our time together and speak with you more casually, knowing the major portion of our learning new things has drawn to a close. I hope you don't mind.

You see, I've spent years trying to find those small but pivotal aspects in life that, when put together, result in great things. In all my travels, in all my conversations with people, in all of my readings, I was always paying attention. I was always searching for the basic elements that were present in what people call success. I mean, if you're going to make a loaf of bread, there's a recipe, right? If you want to build a bird feeder, you should be able to look on the web and find some basic plans and go from there. That's the kind of thing I went searching for, feeling that there just *had to be* some recipe for success.

That's what this entire book is about. It offers a way to start from wherever you are in life, set new goals, and then achieve them!

I've had the rare opportunity not only to speak with thousands of people, but also to read for them as a psychic—thousands of people in more than eighteen different countries around the world! It took me by surprise at first when a person in Sri Lanka asked a question similar to that of a person in London. I mean, seriously, I know that people are people no matter where they are in the world, yet it still shook me a little bit.

Such diverse cultures, so many different social settings, yet the same themes kept repeating over and over. At first, this realization seemed so enormous that it defied thought. You know what I mean? You start to think about something and it turns into a weekend of philosophical conjecture that makes you feel like you're chasing your tail and gaining nothing, except a giant headache from thinking so hard. Yet there was something there, and it was staring me in the eye, daring me to figure it out.

My first inclination was just to keep reading for people and let one of those self-help guru types write a book about a crazy new mystical hocus-pocus kind of deal. Guess what? I did just that, for about three months. You know what happened? It made me feel bad, like I knew could do better. Sure, I was helping people, one reading and conversation at a time, but I *knew* there was more to what I was doing—there was information there that I was letting just go in one ear and out the other, not paying attention. That's what really set me in motion, that feeling, that knowing there was something more.

Here's the funny part that a lot of people don't know about psychics who also happen to be empaths. When I read for people, not only do I see things (pictures, little movies) and hear things (just like someone talking while standing next to me), but I also experience the entire thing emotionally, from the client's point of view. (Similar to internal immersive imagery.) So, if someone has a reading about a relationship issue, I feel what they feel, then I perceive what the insight or information is. I *feel both sides* of the reading. The way it is at the present time and the way it could be in the future. (I say "could be" because the outcome is *always* the choice of the client.)

A cute example: I was reading for a woman in her early thirties once, when out of the blue, her grandmother had a message for me to give her. So, I passed it along. The woman was shocked and said, "Grandma?" All of a sudden, there I was, standing in the middle of this grandmother's kitchen while she was cooking Thanksgiving dinner. The sights, the smells, the emotions, all of it, it was just as though I had been transported to that very time and place. For both the client and me, it was a wonderful experience, as I was able to sit in the kitchen with this loving elderly woman and act as an intermediary in this odd type of conversation. Sitting there and describing the kitchen in detail to my client helped her know it was real, which helped her believe that the words (even the vernacular I was using) were coming from her grandmother. This is often how things work for me; it's an all-encompassing experience. It's not common for me to experience readings this vividly, but when I do, most of the time it is very similar.

I'm using this as an example to show you how I often get to see, hear, and feel (and even sometimes smell) both sides of the reading. This was something that helped me deal with a pile of information that came through in all those years. It helps me provide a more insightful and in-depth reading when I understand why the client is seeking information, as well as perceive the relevant information to relate to my client.

So there I was, on the path of reading for serious reasons, helping many people and experiencing a multitude of situations, questions, and circumstances. I was adding notes to my journal that, at times, made no sense to me at all. Yet, when I looked back at them, they helped fill in some of the blanks, like little pushpins on a road map that make no sense until you take string and connect them all together.

After eight hundred readings, I had compiled a significant amount of information. After five thousand, it was enough to boggle the mind, and I was able to begin to put that knowledge to use when helping other people. When I reached a personal goal of fifteen thousand readings, I knew I had figured it out. It went like this.

I began making notations about broad topics: relationships, finances, careers, health, personal growth. When I had hit the eight-hundred-reading mark, I began to look more in depth at what I was seeing. I had to understand not only the forest but know each tree also. Again, at first look, the task was so daunting I wanted to stop, and just back away from it all. Yet I began to see signs of promise that I could figure it out.

So, one main topic at a time, I sorted information into groups of what worked for people and what did not. When I ran across situations that were similar, I would examine them to see why something would work for one person and not another. What were the differences? Was it a mind-set, a certain level of success attained in life, the amount of money they had? Was it their job that influenced the outcome? I separated my groups of information into a much more complex and organized system. I kept sifting through all of them, looking for those key ingredients that spelled success. When I would find one, I wrote it down. Then I would do the same thing with the other main topics, one at a time, with the same system, all the time writing down my key insights, those things that worked, and why.

Over a period of time, and many headaches later, the common threads began to emerge in my work. I was able to begin to tie a part of success to more than one area of life. I found it would work in career, finances, and relationships. I was thrilled at this point! Then my bubble would burst because it seemed to fail when it hit personal growth or another area of life. So, I would dive back into the groups of information, looking for something I might have missed. Sooner or later, in all my musings, all my time spent in contemplative thought, and even in times of talking with spirit guides, I would find that missing something.

(A side note: I have always been bullheaded when I work with my guides, and I argue a lot with them, thinking I might be right in my thoughts and point of view. In that regard, I am the stereotypical man: stubborn and slow to admit fault. Thankfully my guides have always been loving and patient with me, waiting for the eventual epiphany to hit me like a ton of bricks, and it always does. Then I apologize and go back to work like a giddy kid all over again, knowing something new that helps me along in my work. They never gave me the answers; I had to work for them. One day it did dawn on me that if they had given me all the answers, I might know the information, but I would not truly *understand it*. Therein was the key, *understanding* what I was doing, because without understanding, there was no way I was ever going to be able to help anyone.)

After so many readings, it was all making sense. I was able to see those threads that were common to so many aspects in life. I found the common core portions of what works for people. After years of helping people, I finally had all the ingredients!

Then I realized the next step: making a recipe that people could follow. Sure, I had all the ingredients lined up, but that's like going to the grocery store. Yep, they have all the things for dinner, but unless you have an idea in your mind of *what* is for dinner, you're basically out of luck. You could walk around for hours looking at food and be just as lost as when you walked in, and the longer you looked at it all, the more frustrated you would become. All this food and not a single clue what to make for dinner.

Yes, we've all been there, we all do it. We go to the store and walk around hoping for an idea to come to our mind, then pick up the things we need to fill that shopping list. Funny how we all do it from time to time, isn't it? Now you can imagine how all of us, at one point in time or another, experience the same frustrations in life.

So here I was, a good list of practical information at my fingertips. But how was I going to design a road map to success out of it all? Then I did the unthinkable: I went Einstein! I looked at the whole slew of information and treated it like one of those maze puzzles, where you trace a line from start to finish, and I did what we all do. I started at the finish point of the maze and worked my way backwards to the beginning!

I started with one main topic, like finances. I began with a *success* and worked my way backwards to the very beginning, the issue. (I say issue instead of problem because I used to have a boss that harped on me, "We don't have problems, we have issues! Problems are those things that use mathematics on a chalkboard! Issues are things that have resolutions! We resolve things! So I don't want to hear anyone say we have a problem!" Truthfully, he was a very good boss, and I learned a lot from him.)

When I found a path that worked, going from *success* and working my way to *issue*, I would go through a few hundred readings and see if it really did work. Where it did not, I looked for more information and filled in the gaps. Then, when I had a working template, I would apply it to the next major topic, like relationships.

On and on this went, making a working template, scrapping ideas and thoughts, making new templates. In order for it to be a valid template, it had to fit all four main topics (love, relationship, career, finance). There were times I wanted to throw the whole work out the window, trying to find a unified theory to fit so many aspects of life. In the spring of 2013, I did set my project aside to take a much-needed break for three months while I worked on a guided imagery CD project. When I had completed that recording, I was able to rejoin this entire work again, this time with a renewed sense of vigor and seeing the "light at the end of the tunnel," so to speak. I found I was only a half step away from the finish line, and pressed on.

That half step turned out to be taking the time to find fundamental parts of science, those things we all know and use in life, to help illuminate and effectively convey what I was seeing, experiencing, and grappling with. The understanding of magnetism and polarizing our lives was the very first part of science that melded with the working templates. Taking a slightly different perspective on magnetism helped explain certain key aspects rather well. Finding the other portions of everyday science took only slightly longer, but when I did find them, it all snapped into place. It seemed almost too easy, when I put the results down on paper and used it as a road map of sorts. I looked at my life first, noting points at which I had made pivotal choices, examining the outcomes of those choices, and analyzing how they all fit into my templates, theories, and thoughts. It was rather spooky, at times, looking at my life in a clinical spotlight and seeing results that ran hand-in-hand with my work. However, it did all fit, and it does all work.

The result of all of this is what you are holding in your hands. This guide represents years of thought, speculation, introspection, education, and then putting it to the test. When I surpassed the twenty-thousand-reading mark, I found great satisfaction in knowing that this system, the Einstein Principle, truly works. The rightful question would be: Michael, can you prove it?

Yes. I can. It goes like this:

Five years ago, I put this entire work to the ultimate test. I spoke with my wife, Shelly, and decided to, as they say, walk my talk—trial by fire. It was either going to work, all of it, or I was going to run a wrecking ball through my life. Shelly agreed with me, and more to the point, believed in me like I've never experienced in my life.

Shelly, our two children, and I lived in a small three-bedroom apartment on the main street of town. It was the bottom half of a house, and the upper half was split into two apartments. My family was tripping all over each other, trying to stay out of each other's way. We had moved in to that apartment in order to regain a sense of family closeness and stability. However, in less time than it took to move in, we had already outgrown it. So, I set some ambitious goals: I am going to become a more loving husband, living with my family in a four-bedroom home that has a large yard to play in, and achieving financial security and success.

That was New Year's Eve, 2010.

It is now April of 2015.

We moved into our current home (twenty-four hundred square feet on an acre of land) three and a half years ago. I'm writing to you from the fourth bedroom, which I converted into my office. On the back of the house is a covered patio (pavilion is a more apt description) and a rather large twenty-eight-foot round swimming pool. Shelly and I recently purchased, and paid cash for, our son's car, a gift for his graduation. I also added a brand-new recording booth and studio equipment in my office to record more audio projects. Oh, one more thing. In that five years, we doubled our household income. Twice.

So yes, it does work. I am living proof that it works. I followed the same recipe for success that you have read in this book, and that we have spent time in our conversation discussing.

I did it.

So can you.

All you need to do is apply yourself, believe in yourself, and open yourself to your ideals of a new and incredible life.

Epilogue

I know that an epilogue is designed to be a summation of a written work, but both you and I know I am *not* a creature of conventional habit. Well, maybe there is something else that needs to be addressed, just maybe. And maybe it goes something like this...

What an amazing conversation we've had! For me, personally, I know it ranks right up there with the best of them in my life. For that, I would like to say, "Thank you."

Thank you for spending your time with me.

Thank you for taking time to listen to me expound on my insights.

Thank you for treating our time together with respect.

Thank you for being in the world, helping make it a better place.

Now, it comes time for me to tell you a few things. *<grin>*

Dream your dreams, because now you know you can make them real!

Find your passion, then place your stepping-stones in line to pursue it!

Believe in yourself like never before, and never let anyone tell you otherwise!

Never, ever stop setting new goals and reaching for the stars!

No matter what, until the end of my days, I BELIEVE IN YOU!

—Michael

Appendix

While You Are on Your Way to Success

I'm going to add some things here for you to think about. My hope is that you might find them useful as you "Go Einstein" and embark on your new life!

From some of my seminars I have done, these are what I term the Three Fundamental Understandings.

First Fundamental: The Past is the Past

No matter how many instances there are in life of a desire to rewind an event and have the ability to do it over, it never happens. Once an event has transpired, it's gone, never to come back. This is the first basic concept: The Past is the Past.

I know that almost everyone on the planet understands past, present, and future. Everyone agrees that yesterday is gone, last week is the same way, and we only turn twenty-one once in our lives.

Yet time after time this same issue arises in conversation after conversation, event after event. People know the past is nothing more than a memory or history, yet so many allow their lives to be ruled by it. They allow something that is over and done to rule their life like an emperor, dictating how they will conduct themselves. This type of thought and behavior is something that needs to be eradicated in our lives in order to focus on the future and our success.

Here is one way to look at things that have happened. The past is nothing more than a series of choices we have made and actions we have taken. Those choices and actions have placed us where we are today, at this very moment.

The hard truth: there is not a single thing we can do to change the past, and we all know it. We cannot take back the words which caused a fight with our spouse, we cannot undo the action of eating an extra portion of ice cream causing us to gain those additional pounds.

At the same time, we must not let that argument with our spouse create a roadblock to building a stronger and more loving relationship with them. We should not look in the mirror and berate ourselves because we are overweight; we simply need to set our resolve and change our eating habits to reflect who we are going to become. We cannot allow the thought of "It is too late to change" to creep into our mind; we can make changes now and perfect who we are.

The past is nothing more than a reminder of the things we did. We did some things very correctly, while we might have royally screwed up in some other areas of life. No matter what has happened, the past is personal history, something to review and help us determine if we desire to experience the same outcomes or not.

Second Fundamental: My Life, My Responsibility

Continuing from a constructive perspective on the past comes the next fundamental understanding, accepting one hundred percent responsibility for who we are. For many people, this is one of the harder concepts to apply. Many people spend much of their time finding fault or blaming someone or something else, trying to erase the burden of personal responsibility.

The thing is, it never works. It only leads to more of the same. Putting this fundamental into words, it would read this way: My life and current situations are a direct result of my thoughts, choices, actions, and reactions.

There is no bogeyman that coerced us to argue with our loved one, there was no one twisting our arms when we ate more than we should have, there was no law stating we could not have continuing education in life. Everything we are in our lives is a direct result of the choices we have made.

Placing blame on an outside person, event, situation, or anything else is nothing more than a form of denial or escapism. By doing so, we will never take the necessary steps to create meaningful change or take steps to create success in life. Playing the "Blame Game" might make you feel better, yet it will never help solve the problem. Being anything but responsible for who we are, as well as where we are, is only allowing outside influence to control our lives.

Yet we should not ever take this to an extreme. Being responsible for our thoughts and actions is one thing. Continuously blaming ourselves for failures is also self-defeating, and will cause inner turmoil, self-doubt, regret, and a host of other issues.

If something has happened, simply realize where you were responsible in the event or situation. Doing so will allow us to make changes and continue on our road to success. Being responsible in our daily lives results in self-empowerment and gives us clarity about who we truly are. It allows us to exercise choice, to make changes, to constantly strengthen our vision of where we are going and why.

One of the ways I help people with the aspect of personal responsibility is with a simple sentence: This life you are living is all about you. It is not an egocentric statement, rather the opening statement to an entire understanding.

Think about these things:

- When the electric bill comes for your house or apartment, does it have your neighbor's name on it, or yours?
- When you put your clothes on this morning, who decided what shoes you would wear?
- When you take time to read a book, who decides what genre to read?

- If you are driving and going faster than the speed limit, then are pulled over by an officer of the law, do they write the ticket for anyone else but you?
- Who controls the words that come out of your mouth or are texted, posted, or written down on paper by you?

Every aspect of your life reflects what you think, how you react to things, how you interact with other people, how you live your life. Being responsible for our lives will only empower us to do more of what we desire and spend less effort dealing with those experiences we do not want.

Third Fundamental: On or Off

The third fundamental understanding relates to how things are in your life. No matter what the topic is, everything in life is either present, or it is not. Saying that there are a lot of gray areas in life is avoidance. Everything has a yes or no to it.

Your vehicle either has a flat tire or it does not. Saying it has a slow leak means it will eventually become flat, not that it is. Saying it has a slow leak means you are aware that there is an issue. Are you going to do something to fix the issue, or not? Putting more air in the tire might help for a short amount of time, but it does not fix, or resolve, the current issue, does it?

The same yes or no statement can be applied to our financial structure. A very simple question, do you have enough money? The answer is either yes or no. If you find yourself saying maybe, then you might need to examine the amount needed and ask yourself again. Saying, "I might have enough money" more than likely means you do not really know, which is going to result in something you do not want. You either have enough money to pay the bills, or you do not. Likewise, you either have enough money to purchase the new television, or you do not. Saying maybe often leads to trouble.

People often raise questions about being in the middle of something and trying to answer yes or no. One of the most common points brought up is being in the middle of a diet, and trying to answer yes or no to a goal. I respond like this:

- Is a weight goal set? They answer yes.
- Are they working on the diet? For real? They say yes. (Sometimes with a grin.)
- Have they lost weight to this date? They say yes.
- Has the goal been achieved? Most answer no.
- Does this mean the diet failed? A short pause for thought, then a tentative no is given.
- Is the diet still going? Are you still working on your goal? Yes and yes.
- So a goal was set, measurable progress has been made, continued progress is underway, and there has not been a failure. Is all this correct? Most answer yes.

When something complex comes into our lives, or we are working on long-range goals, it is even more important to break things down into the basic component parts. This allows a person the ability to reach that simple answer.

This is such an important tool in our journey to success, the ability to define yes or no, have or have not. It is a simple statement that addresses whatever we are facing at any given time in our lives. Asking ourselves questions and allowing simple definitive answers continues to empower us and move toward our desires and goals. Cut through the "maybe" and get to the real answer, yes or no. Finding the simple answer will result in self-confidence, clarity of thought, and peace of mind. To have that in your life means a job well done!

www.ingramcontent.com/pod-product-compliance
Lightning Source LLC
Chambersburg PA
CBHW071636050426

42443CB00028B/3338